Open

The All-Time Book of Fascinating Facts

And Find Out:

**Since there's no ham in hamburgers —
why do we call them hamburgers**

**What are all the many amazing coincidences between
the assassinations of Presidents John Kennedy and
Abraham Lincoln**

Why are police officers called cops

**What do the "O" and "K" stand for in the
expression "OK"**

**The incredible fact that three of the first five U.S.
presidents all died on July 4th**

And much more!

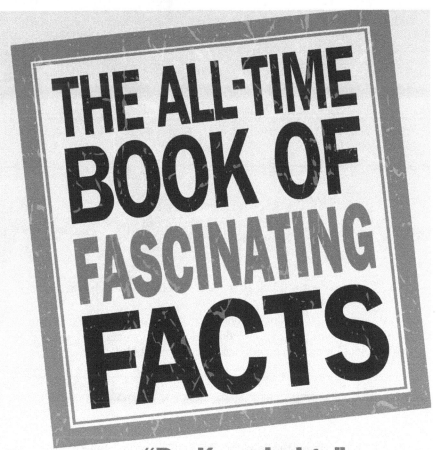

THE ALL-TIME BOOK OF FASCINATING FACTS

"Dr. Knowledge"
Charles Reichblum

Knowledge in a Nutshell Inc.

Paperbacks

For inquires or information, or to order more printed books or ebooks, contact Knowledge in a Nutshell Inc., 1420 Centre Ave., Suite 2213, Pittsburgh PA 15219, or go to knowledgeinanutshell.com, or call 1-800-NUTSHELL.

How could a person be born in both Florida AND Missouri?

There was a person born in Florida AND Missouri—and he was famous.

Here's how this oddity happened to author Mark Twain:

It was in a small town in northeast Missouri named Florida that Twain was born in 1835. That town was Florida, Missouri. So he was born in Florida and Missouri.

Maybe you could win a bet someday by betting someone you know how a person really could be born in both Florida and Missouri.

What famous sports event was named by a little girl?

Hard to believe, but the Super Bowl owes its name to an 8-year-old girl.

After the merger of the National Football League and the American Football League in 1966, football owners were deciding what to call their new championship game.

One afternoon, while sitting in his living room, Lamar Hunt, who owned the Kansas City Chiefs, was on the telephone, talking with other owners on a conference call, discussing proposed names for the championship game. While the conversation was going on, Hunt's 8-year-old daughter Sharron was on the living room floor playing with a popular toy at the time, a black rubber ball called a "super ball." From that she got the idea to suggest to her dad that the football owners name their title game the "Super Bowl" after the "super ball." Lamar Hunt smiled, told other owners of his daughter's idea, and, lo and behold, that became the name of the game.

So the famous Super Bowl really owes its name to a little girl.

There's no ham in hamburgers—so why do we call them hamburgers?

To answer the question as to why we call them hamburgers even though they have no ham in them, you have to go back to the late 1800s when a large number of German immigrants came to the United States.

Among the immigrants were people from the city of Hamburg, Germany. They brought with them their custom of serving ground meat.

That kind of meat was soon named after their city, Hamburg, and that's how hamburgers got their name—from their city of origin. But the next time you have a hamburger, realize there is no ham in hamburgers.

What man—incredibly—was on the scene when THREE U.S. presidents were assassinated?

That amazing fate befell Abraham Lincoln's son Robert. Robert was with his father right after Abraham Lincoln was fatally shot in 1865—and that was the start of an unbelievable streak.

Sixteen years later, in 1881, Robert Lincoln had become a member of the cabinet in President James Garfield's administration and was standing with Garfield when Garfield was fatally shot at a Washington railroad station.

Twenty years after that, in 1901, Robert had become head of the U.S. Chamber of Commerce, and was invited by President William McKinley to join him at a business exposition in Buffalo, N.Y. Robert walked into the exhibition hall just as McKinley was fatally shot.

After that, Robert Lincoln vowed never to get anywhere near a U.S. president again. Unlikely he would have been invited anyhow.

Surprise--what's the eastern-most U.S. state?

Crazy as it sounds, Alaska is BOTH the western-most AND the eastern-most state of the United States.

No surprise that Alaska is the western-most state—but here's why it's also the eastern-most.

Part of the Aleutian Islands of Alaska extend so far west, they actually cross the line that divides the Eastern Hemisphere and the Western Hemisphere of the world.

So, because part of Alaska extends into the Eastern Hemisphere, geographers say that technically makes Alaska both the western-most and eastern-most U.S. state.

Not only all that, but Alaska is also, of course, the northern-most state, too.

It's been said that more people in America know the words to this song than any other song. What is that song?

Surprisingly, this song that just about everybody knows, wasn't written by any professional song writer. It was written by two school-teaching sisters in Kentucky, Mildred and Patty Hill.

The song is... "Happy Birthday To You".

Mildred and Patty wrote the song for kids in their classes—except originally they called it "Good Morning To All". It was meant to be a classroom greeting as the kids came to school. But then, one day, when one of the pupils had a birthday, Mildred and Patty changed the words from "Good Morning To All" to "Happy Birthday To You"—and history was made.

Today, virtually everyone from kids on up know the words to "Happy Birthday To You".

Why are police officers called cops?

There are several theories on why police officers are called cops, but the one that is thought to be the most plausible is this one:

In the 19th century, it was a tradition for many police officers to wear copper badges and copper buttons on their uniforms. People then started referring to police officers as "coppers" because you'd always see the copper badge or copper buttons when a police officer came into view, and people would say, "Here comes the copper."

As time went on, people shortened the word "copper" to "cop."

Amazingly, about one-third of all the people in the world live in just 2 countries. What are those 2 countries that have about one-third of the Earth's population?

The total population in the world is near 8 billion—but about 1.4 billion people live in China and about 1.3 in India, so China's and India's population together is about 2.7 billion, or about one-third of the Earth's population.

Why didn't any football or baseball team play the national anthem at any game before the 1930s?

It's hard to believe now, but if you had gone to any football or baseball game—or any other game—before the 1930s, you would not have heard the national anthem.

The reason is that the United States had no national anthem until 1931!

Finally, in that year, Congress adopted "The Star-Spangled Banner" as the national anthem and it was signed into law by President Herbert Hoover.

Another interesting fact is that "The Star-Spangled Banner" was written in 1814 and it took 117 years until it was made the national anthem.

Why do people wear their wedding ring on the third finger of the left hand?

It's the custom in the U.S. and some other countries to wear the wedding ring on the third finger of the left hand—but why is that? Why aren't wedding rings worn on some other finger?

The tradition of wearing a wedding ring only on the third finger of the left hand began with an old belief that the nerve in that finger runs directly to the heart—and so people have been wearing wedding rings on that same finger on the left hand in all the years since.

On the other hand (if you'll excuse the pun), there are countries where people wear their wedding ring on their right hand. That's true in such countries as Russia, Poland, Greece, Germany, India and Spain. One theory on why they do that is the belief that since most people are right-handed, the wedding ring would be more noticeable on the right hand.

What person who couldn't read or write as a teenager, grew up to be president of the United States?

Andrew Johnson never went to school. As a young boy, he went to work to help support his family. When he was 17, he still couldn't read or write.

Then, his girlfriend, 16-year-old Eliza McCardle began to teach him to read and write. Little did she know by doing that, she would someday become first lady of the land. But that's what happened.

Andrew and Eliza got married as teenagers, and then in his 20s, the newly literate Andrew went into politics and became mayor of his small town of Greeneville, Tenn. A few years later he was elected to the state legislature, then became governor of Tennessee, and eventually a member of the U.S. Congress.

In 1864, when Republican President Abraham Lincoln was preparing to run for a second term, he wanted a Southern Democrat as his running mate to help unify the country after the Civil War, and Lincoln selected Andrew Johnson as his vice presidential nominee. The Lincoln-Johnson ticket won the election, and then in early1865, Lincoln was assassinated.

At that point, Vice President Andrew Johnson—the teenager who couldn't read or write—became the president of the United States, with Eliza as first lady.

Which major league baseball team had a priest, a nun and a saint playing for them?

It was the Cincinnati Reds.

They had a player named Eddie Priest in 1998, a player named Howie Nunn in 1961 and 1962, and a player named Randy St. Claire in 1988.

The Reds also had a church and a temple playing for them—Bubba Church in 1952 and 1953, and Johnny Temple from 1952 to 1959.

On which 2 days of the year do Americans eat the most food?

According to several surveys, the No. 1 eating day for Americans is Thanksgiving Day.

And, the No. 2 day when Americans eat the most is Super Bowl Sunday, which is also the biggest pizza-eating day.

What are the many eerie coincidences between the assassinations of Abraham Lincoln and John Kennedy?

We get more requests from our CBS listeners for this story than any other:

Both Kennedy and Lincoln were shot on a Friday.

Each was sitting next to his wife when shot. Neither wife was injured.

Their last names—Kennedy and Lincoln—both have seven letters.
.
Lincoln was elected to Congress in 1846, Kennedy in 1946.

Lincoln was elected president in 1860, Kennedy in 1960.

Both were succeeded by a man named Johnson—Lincoln by Andrew Johnson, and Kennedy by Lyndon Johnson.

Andrew Johnson was born in 1808, Lyndon Johnson in 1908.

Each Johnson's first and last names together are composed of 13 letters.

The assassins of Lincoln and Kennedy were both known by three names—John Wilkes Booth and Lee Harvey Oswald.

The names of both John Wilkes Booth and Lee Harvey Oswald are each composed of 15 letters.

Booth shot Lincoln in a theater and hid in a warehouse. Oswald shot Kennedy from a warehouse and hid in a theater.

Both Booth and Oswald were killed before they could be brought to trial.

Lincoln had sons named Robert and Edward. Kennedy had brothers named Robert and Edward.

Lincoln's secretary was named Kennedy. Kennedy's secretary was named Lincoln.

And the final coincidence: The car in which Kennedy was riding when he was shot was… a Lincoln.

Why are Democratic states called blue states and Republican states called red states?

Some newspapers and TV networks began this whole thing by coloring states on their maps showing election results—but for a while, different networks and papers used red and blue interchangeably, and there was no general agreement that Democratic states should be blue and Republican states red.

Finally, for the 2000 presidential election, the media got together and decided to standardize the colors to avoid confusion.

It was agreed to adopt the policy of a graphics man at the New York Times who said he chose red for Republican states and blue for Democratic states because Republican and red both start with "R." It was as simple as that—and, by the way, a good way to remember it.

How did Sylvan Goldman change the way we shop?

Although most folks today have never heard of Sylvan Goldman, he invented something that's used by millions of shoppers now every week.

Goldman owned a grocery store in Oklahoma City in the 1930s, and noticed that customers weren't buying as many items as they might because they couldn't carry them all to the checkout counter. In those days, some shoppers brought their own baskets with them to the store, but those baskets quickly became too heavy or too full.

Sylvan Goldman solved the problem.

He invented the supermarket shopping cart in 1937, got a patent on it, and became a millionaire.

Goldman's shopping cart soon was being used by stores everywhere, and he changed the way we shop.

Why are the music awards called the Grammys?

No, they're not named after somebody's grandmother.

The Grammy awards got their name from the word "gramophone," which was a type of early phonographs that played recorded music.

When the Grammy awards were begun in the 1950s, the original idea was to name them the Eddies after Thomas Edison, the man who invented the phonograph.

But at the last minute, organizers changed the name to Grammys, so Thomas Edison lost out in having the music awards named after him.

What's the coincidence between the crew of the first men on the moon—and the first men on Earth?

The crew of Apollo 11, which put the first men on the moon, was Neil Armstrong, Buzz Aldrin and Michael Collins whose last-name initials are A-A-C—Armstrong, Aldrin and Collins.

The Biblical first men on Earth were Adam, Abel and Cain—also with the initials A-A-C.

Now, that's an interesting coincidence.

There are 8 countries in the world—all well known—whose names all start with the letter "I". What are those 8 countries?

The eight countries whose names start with "I" are, in alphabetical order, Iceland, India, Indonesia, Iran, Iraq, Ireland, Israel and Italy.

You might want to include a ninth country, Ivory Coast, but that nation prefers to be known as Cote d'Ivoire and they have officially changed their name from Ivory Coast to the French version of its name, Cote d'Ivoire.

For what holiday was the song "Jingle Bells" written?

Surprisingly, although we hear the song "Jingle Bells" a lot at Christmas time, it was originally written, not for Christmas, but for another holiday—and if you listen to all the words, there's no mention of Christmas anywhere in "Jingle Bells."

"Jingle Bells" was written by James Pierpont in 1857 for a church event in Boston that was being held at Thanksgiving time.

Check all the words—they're about "dashing through the snow in a one-horse open sleigh." Nothing about Christmas is ever mentioned.

But you can enjoy it at Christmas time anyway.

What words have unnecessary letters in them?

It's surprising how many words in the English language have unnecessary letters.

For example, how about the word "psychology." We don't need that letter "p" at the beginning. We don't pronounce the "p." The word "knock"—what's that first "k" doing there? We don't pronounce that first "k." Do we need the "e" at the end of "have"? Why is there an "o" in "jeopardy"? What about the "b" in the word doubtful? Why is there a "u" in "guilt"? What's "w" doing in front of the word "wrong"? How about the "ugh" in "bought"? The word is pronounced "bot," so we don't need those "ugh" letters. And why in the world is there an "s" in "island"?

That just scratches the surface. You might enjoy thinking of so many more everyday words that have unnecessary letters.

Is it true that 3 of the first 5 U.S. presidents all died on July 4?

In an amazing coincidence, three of the first five U.S. presidents did indeed all die on July 4.

John Adams, the second president, and Thomas Jefferson, the third president, both died on the same July 4—July 4, 1826. Adams died in Quincy, Mass., and Jefferson in Charlottesville, Va.

And then, incredibly, the fifth president, James Monroe, also died on July 4—July 4, 1831. Monroe died in New York City.

What are the odds that three of the first five presidents would all die—of unrelated causes—on the same date, and that date, of all dates, would be July 4.

How really big is the White House—how many rooms are there?

It doesn't look that big from the outside, but here's what exists in the White House:

There are 132 rooms, 35 bathrooms, 412 doors, 147 windows, 8 staircases, 3 elevators plus a tennis court, a jogging track, a single lane bowling alley, a putting green, a swimming pool and a movie theater.

Here's an easy-looking test that many people miss— count the number of "F's" in the sentence below. How many are there?

"FINISHED FILES ARE THE RESULT OF YEARS OF SCIENTIFIC STUDY COMBINED WITH THE EXPERIENCE OF YEARS."

The human brain tends to skip over and miss all the "F's" in that sentence. Most people get three or four "F's"—but there are six.

Why are the points in tennis scored as 15, 30 and 40 instead of simply 1, 2 and 3?

The unusual scoring in tennis started back in the early days of the game when they used the face of clocks as scoreboards—and moved the hands of the clock to 15 after the hour for the first point, 30 after for the second, and 45 after for the third—so the points became 15, 30 and 45.

Later, many players began to change the 45 to 40 to give us today's 15, 30 and 40, but not 1, 2 and 3.

How old do you have to be to serve in the U.S. Congress, or be president, or be on the U.S. Supreme Court?

According to the Constitution, a person must be at least 25 years old to serve in the U.S. House of Representatives, and must be at least 30 years old to be a U.S. senator.

To be president of the United States, a person must be at least 35 years of age.

As far as the U.S. Supreme Court goes, there is, according to the Constitution, no age requirement.

How did the Nasdaq stock market get that name— why is it called Nasdaq?

There was no Nasdaq on the financial markets for many years. Nasdaq wasn't founded until 1971, and it quickly became a major player in the buying and selling of stocks.

But even some people who buy and sell on Nasdaq aren't quite sure why it's called Nasdaq.

Nasdaq got its name from the first letters of National Association Securities Dealers Automated Quotations—N-a-s-d-a-q.

Is it really true that the current 50-star U.S. flag was designed by a 17-year-old high school student?

When preparations were being made in the late 1950s for Hawaii to join the Union as the 50th state, it was obvious that the nation would need a new flag. The flag, of course, has as many stars as there are states—and with Hawaii coming in, the flag would have to be updated.

For many years, the U.S. had 48 states and the 48-star flag had a nice, neat design, with 6 even rows of 8 stars each. Then Alaska became the 49th state and again the flag had a nice, neat design with 7 rows of 7 stars each. **But with Hawaii becoming the 50th state, how would you add 1 star to that even design?**

President Eisenhower announced a national contest, inviting entries for the design of the new flag—and how the 50 stars should be positioned.

A high school teacher in Lancaster, Ohio, Stanley Pratt, decided to make ideas for designing the new flag a class project. One of his students, 17-year-old Robert Heft, came up with a design showing nine rows of alternating lengths—6 stars on the top row, 5 stars on the second row, 6 stars on the third row, 5 stars on the fourth row, 6 stars on the fifth row, 5 stars on the sixth row, 6 stars on the seventh row, 5 stars on the eighth row, and 6 stars on the ninth row. Add that up, and it's 50 stars.

Teacher Pratt gave Robert Heft a B- for that design. But Robert asked his teacher that if, by any wild chance his design would be accepted, would Pratt then change his grade to an A? Pratt, perhaps laughing to himself, and perhaps thinking that this high school kid's chances of winning were near zero, agreed to give him an A if the unexpected happened.

Thousands of designs from around the country were submitted to President Eisenhower, with all different kinds of ways to position the 50 stars. You can probably guess what happened. Eisenhower, with the advice of the committee he had formed, chose the design like the one Robert had submitted. Others also submitted that design but it's a true story that today's 50-star flag is exactly like the one designed by 17-year-old Robert Heft.

And, what happened to Robert Heft? Did he get that A? The answer is yes. His teacher kept his word and changed his grade. Then, it turns out that Robert, himself, became a high school teacher and later a college professor. After his teaching career, he became the mayor of Napoleon, Ohio. He died in 2009 at age 67.

Many Americans get a good feeling when they look at the U.S. flag—but imagine the special thrill Robert Heft got every time he looked at the flag during his adult years—with his design of the stars.

Why is the Academy Award statue called an Oscar?

Originally, the Academy Award statue had no name, but one day in the 1930s, the executive director of the Academy, Margaret Herrick, looked at the statue and said, "You know, that looks like my Uncle Oscar"—actually a man named Oscar Pierce.

She began referring to the statue as "Oscar," and the Hollywood press picked up on it. They liked the idea of the statue having a name, and so they began calling it Oscar—and the name stuck and spread.

A twist to the story is that the man whose name is on the biggest movie award of all had nothing to do with the movies himself. Oscar Pierce was a farmer in Texas—but his first name lives on in movie annals.

Why didn't Paul Revere say, "The British are coming"?

Here's a correction of one of the biggest myths in American history that has lingered down through the years—that one about Paul Revere riding through the countryside on the eve of the Revolutionary War, shouting, "The British are coming, the British are coming."

Upon further review, he never would have said that, and here's why.

The people Paul Revere were warning were predominately British themselves—they were still British colonists—so he never would have said "The British are coming." What he did yell was, "The regulars are coming," meaning regular troops of the British army.

The British army was referred to then as the regulars. "The regulars are coming," Revere yelled, not "The British are coming."

Why do we call them bathrooms?

Ever stop to think that many places that we call bathrooms have no baths in them—yet we still call them bathrooms.   People in restaurants or stores or theaters or offices say they're going to the bathroom, but those places have no baths, and even some rooms in homes that we call bathrooms have no baths.

By the same token, the word "rest room" is often used—but people don't generally go in there to rest. Maybe we should use different names.

The reason the words bathrooms and rest rooms are used is because they sound a little better than "toilet rooms."

It's amazing how many sports there are in which the second letter of the name of the sport is an "o". Which sports are those?

There's football, golf, hockey, boxing, soccer, horse racing, bowling, pool, motor sports, softball, mountain climbing, polo, rowing, bocce, bobsled, roller skating, pole vaulting, boating, and volleyball, to name some of them.

There's no reason for it, but it's just a coincidence how many sports have names in which the second letter of their name is an "o."

Which U.S. state no longer exists?

There once was a state named Franklin—named after Benjamin Franklin. It was between North Carolina and Tennessee.

The state of Franklin lasted for four years after the Revolutionary War, but all kinds of political and land disputes erupted, and the state of Franklin went out of business. Its land became part of what is now eastern Tennessee.

There is one reminder today. There's a road in eastern Tennessee called the State of Franklin highway—part of a road that used to go into the state of Franklin.

Meantime, poor Benjamin Franklin. This great Founding Father deserved to have a state named after him—and did—but doesn't anymore.

Who were teddy bears named after?

U.S. president Teddy Roosevelt loved to hunt and was invited by some friends to go on a bear-hunting trip during his presidency in the early 1900s.

His hosts wanted to make sure he had a bear to shoot at, but the only bear they could find for him was a cub, and the president refused to shoot it.

The story appeared in newspapers about how the president spared the cub's life. That story inspired Rose and Morris Michtom who owned a toy store in Brooklyn, N.Y.

They created a little stuffed bear and put it in the window of their store alongside a sign that read: "Teddy's Bear." That was the beginning. The teddy bear was born, and then more and more were made and sold.

An addendum to the story. After the Michtoms sold the first teddy bears, Morris Michtom wrote Teddy Roosevelt and asked permission to call the bears "teddy bears." Roosevelt wrote back and said that would be fine. But reports are that he never got any royalties on his namesake.

What man in jail got almost a million votes for U.S. president?

Can it be—a man in prison got almost one-million votes to be president of the United States?

Yes, it really happened. In the 1920 presidential election, Eugene Debs ran on a third-party Socialist ticket against Republican Warren Harding and Democrat James Cox.

Debs got 919,799 votes despite the fact that he was in the Atlanta Penitentiary at the time, serving a 10-year sentence for violating the Espionage Act. He had been convicted for his actions in opposing the U.S. entry in World War I.

Eugene Debs spent the entire presidential campaign of 1920 in the penitentiary. Harding won the election, but almost a million people voted for prisoner Debs in one of the strangest elections in U.S. history.

There really was a man named Nacho who gave nachos their name. Who was Nacho?

Nacho was the manager of a restaurant in Piedras Negras, Mexico, just across the border from Eagle Pass, Texas. His real name was Ignacio Anaya, but everyone called him Nacho which is a nickname for Ignacio.

One night, a group of American tourists came into his restaurant just as Nacho was about to close. Nacho didn't want to turn the group away, but he was low on food to make full dinners, so he improvised and cut up a bunch of tortilla chips, sprinkled them with cheese and jalapeno peppers and popped them into an oven. The tourists loved them, and Nacho realized he might have something. He made them a specialty of his place, and folks throughout southern Texas began going over to Nacho's restaurant to get some of those "nachos." Then, their popularity—and the name—began spreading elsewhere.

Who gave Irving Berlin the inspiration for the song, "God Bless America"?

There's a beautiful story on how Irving Berlin got the idea for the song, "God Bless America."

When Irving Berlin was a child, he and his family had come to America as immigrants from Russia. Irving would often hear his mother say," God bless America"—so happy and thankful was she to be in America.

When he became an adult and a successful songwriter, Berlin often thought of his mother and all the times she had said," God bless America." That gave him the inspiration—and the title—for one of his greatest songs.

Which 3 U.S. states were named after women?

A few states sound as if they might have been named after women—states like Georgia, North and South Carolina, and Louisiana, but they weren't.

Georgia was named for England's King George II. The Carolinas got their name from the Latin version of England's King Charles I's name. And Louisiana wasn't named for anybody named Louise, but for France's King Louis XIV.

The three states that were named for women are Maryland, after Queen Maria of England, and Virginia and West Virginia, named for England's Queen Elizabeth I, known as the Virgin Queen.

What was the most famous newspaper headline of all time?

The most famous headline, according to many journalism people, was a headline that didn't appear in a regular daily newspaper, but one that was in the show business paper, Variety. The headline ran in their July 17, 1935 issue, and is still discussed in journalism classes and show business circles:

Variety, known for special show biz lingo, was running a story about how movie goers in rural areas in the mid-1930s were getting more sophisticated and were getting tired of simple films about farm dramas and rural life. Variety's classic front page headline over that story was: STICKS NIX HICK PIX, meaning people in rural areas (the sticks) were saying no (nix) to unsophisticated (hick) pictures (pix).

Another classic Variety's headline came in the issue of Oct. 30, 1929, a day after the stock market crashed, ushering in the Great Depression. If a show or movie got bad reviews, Variety would say it laid an egg. Variety's front page headline after the stock market crash was WALL ST. LAYS AN EGG.

We say "a.m." for mornings and "p.m." for afternoons, but what do those initials stand for— and why don't we use different initials?

Both "a.m." and "p.m." are Latin abbreviations, with "a.m." standing for "ante meridiem," which means "before noon" in Latin, and "p.m." stands for "post meridiem," which means "after noon" in Latin.

Which raises the question: Why don't we just use English and say "before noon" and "after noon," and use the abbreviations "b.n" and "a.n."?

Are tomatoes fruits or vegetables?

Would you believe, the U.S. Supreme Court once got involved in this question?

Technically, fruits have seeds and vegetables usually don't, but the Supreme Court got involved with tomatoes when Congress passed a tariff on imported vegetables in 1883. A food wholesaler brought tomatoes in from the West Indies and was assessed the tariff. He sued, saying tomatoes are fruits because they have seeds, and therefore are not vegetables, and he should not have to pay the tariff.

The case reached the Supreme Court which said botanically the importer was right. Tomatoes are fruits because they have seeds, BUT the court then ruled that since tomatoes are usually served with the meal and not as a dessert, tomatoes should be considered a vegetable.

So, to answer this question legally, you can say tomatoes are vegetables, not fruits.

Can there be any year without a Friday the 13th?

We can't escape a Friday the 13th. The way our calendars are sequenced, there's at least one Friday the 13th every year.

Any month that starts on a Sunday will have a Friday the 13th and there's at least one of those months every year.

What cities or towns have the name of a land animal or fish or bird in their name?

Here are a few for you to get you started:

There's Buffalo, N.Y.; Beaver, Utah; Cape Cod, Mass.; Chihuahua, Mexico; Eagle Pass, Texas; Moose Jaw, Canada; Oyster Bay, N.Y.; Pompano Beach, Fla.; Elk Grove Village, Ill.; Foxboro, Mass.; Spearfish, S.D.; and Sturgeon Bay, Wisc.

Then there's Phoenix, Ariz.   Phoenix was the legendary bird in mythology that rose from the ashes.

And there's one historic town with two animal names—the place where the Wright Brothers made their first airplane flight—Kitty Hawk, N.C.

What show business people have been elected to high government offices?

It all started with Broadway actress Helen Gahagan Douglas who was elected to the U.S. House of Representatives from California in 1944. Then George Murphy, a song-and-dance man in many movies was elected to the U.S. Senate from California. A fellow movie actor by the name of Ronald Reagan was elected governor of California, then president of the United States, and the trend continued.

TV and movie actor Fred Thompson was elected to the U.S. Senate from Tennessee, actor-singer Sonny Bono was elected to the U.S. House from California, actor Arnold Schwarzenegger became governor of California, and former Saturday Night Live personality Al Franken has been elected to the U.S. Senate from Minnesota.

What are the coincidences of the number 11 and the 9/11 terrorist attacks on the United States on Sept. 11, 2001?

The first plane to hit the World Trade Center in New York on 9/11 was Flight…11.

On Flight 11, there were 92 people on board. 9 + 2 equals…11.

The words "New York City" have exactly…11 letters.

Another plane hit the Pentagon. The words, "The Pentagon" have exactly…11 letters.

Original groundbreaking for construction of the Pentagon took place in 1941 on…Sept. 11.

The Pennsylvania town nearest to where another plane with terrorists crashed is Shanksville. Number of letters in Shanksville…11.

The president of the US at the time, George W. Bush…11 letters in that name.

The Twin Towers in New York, standing side by side, looked like the number…11.

After Sept. 11, there are exactly 111 days left in the year.

When did pizza become popular in the United States?

It's hard to believe now, but there was a time when, in most places in the United States, there were no pizza shops, no pizza delivery and most Americans never ate pizza.

In the years before World War II, what little pizza there was in the U.S. was largely confined to Italian neighborhoods in big cities. In most of the rest of the country, there was no pizza.

That didn't begin to change until after World War II when American servicemen and women returning from being stationed in Italy, brought home the demand for pizza, and pizza's popularity only then began to grow.

What's the only country ever kicked out of the U.N.?

Taiwan was an original member of the United Nations, but Mainland China which still considers Taiwan part of its country and not an independent country, managed to get enough support to have Taiwan expelled from the U.N. in 1971.

Thus, Taiwan has become the only country ever ejected from the U.N., even though many consider it a functioning independent nation.

Of the 196 independent countries in the world, only two others are not in the U.N.—The Vatican which chooses on its own not to be a member (although it does have an observer there), and Kosovo whose independence has not been recognized by all countries and therefore has not yet been a member.

How did the White House almost become the Red House?

If Thomas Jefferson had had his way, the White House would be called the Red House today.

Jefferson wanted the home for U.S. presidents to be built with red bricks—but his idea was over-ridden at the last minute, and a design by Irish-born architect James Hoban was picked instead. Hoban used the home of an Irish duke as the basis for the design of the White House—without red bricks.

It's surprising that Jefferson's idea was defeated. Among other things, he was a noted, respected architect himself who designed his own beautiful home, Monticello, plus the Virginia capitol building and buildings at the University of Virginia.

But just think: If Jefferson's red-brick plan for the president's home had been adopted, the White House would have been called the Red House all these years.

Why is a bullpen in baseball called a bullpen?

There are several theories but most baseball historians say calling it a bullpen started in the early 1900s when the Bull Durham Tobacco Company had advertising signs in lots of ballparks in the area where pitchers warm up—and those signs had a big picture of a bull on them.

Because those signs with a bull on them were in the area where pitchers warm up, people started calling it a bullpen, and that name bullpen has lasted all these years.

What war was named after somebody's ear?

This was a war with a strange name.

There really was a war between two major nations called "The War of Jenkins Ear." It was between England and Spain. And, no kidding, that was the war's name.

In 1731, Spanish sailors boarded an English ship that had docked without permission at an American port that the Spanish believed they controlled. During an ensuing scuffle between Spanish and English sailors, somebody cut off the ear of Robert Jenkins, the captain of the English ship.

There was tension then anyway between Spain and England over which country had access to various ports in the Americas, and the cutting off of Capt. Jenkins' ear whipped up war fever in the English parliament. Soon, war was declared and the war was called "The War of Jenkins Ear."

The war lasted a few years until Spain and England worked out compromises on access to their colonies in America. But the War of Jenkins Ear goes down in history as the war with the most bizarre name of all time.

The introduction to a very famous Christmas song is hardly ever heard—but here it is. What song do these words introduce?

The seldom-heard introduction starts: "The sun is shining, the grass is green, the orange and palm trees sway. There's never been such a day in Beverly Hills, L.A.. But it's December, and…."

Can you guess what's next?

It's… "I'm Dreaming of a White Christmas." That's the song Irving Berlin was writing while he was in Los Angeles doing the music for the movie "Holiday Inn"—the movie in which the song "White Christmas" was introduced in 1942.

Bing Crosby's recording of "White Christmas" still holds the record as the best-selling single record of all time.

What was the strange mystery of Mary Celeste?

Mary Celeste was the name of an American cargo ship that left New York one day in 1872, headed for Italy. It never made it. Weeks later, the ship was discovered drifting along in the Atlantic with no one on board. Its captain and crew of 14 had completely vanished.

There was no sign of foul play, bad weather, violence or any disaster having hit the ship. There was no indication that people like pirates might have boarded the ship because the cargo was untouched. The crew's valuables were still on board, and there was no evidence that any fighting might have taken place.

Along with that, there appeared no reason for the crew to have to abandon ship. There was still a good supply of food and water. The ship was in fine sea-worthy condition. Everything was in place, except the captain and all crew members who had simply disappeared.

They were never found, and to this day, no one knows what happened. The story of the Mary Celeste remains one of the great mysteries of the sea.

What people have the name of a U.S. state as part of their name?

There's film character Indiana Jones
Football Hall of Famer Joe Montana
Novelist Virginia Woolf
Pool player Minnesota Fats
Educator Booker T. Washington
Playwright Tennessee Williams
And, from music fame, Sweet Georgia Brown.

We've all heard of ESPN—but what do those letters ESPN stand for?

The ESPN network was founded in 1979, and the name came from the first letters of the phrase Entertainment and Sports Programming Network.

The network was founded in Bristol, Conn., originally just to telecast local events in their area, but they gradually expanded to covering many sports worldwide.

What amazing thing happens when you multiply numbers by 9?

Here's a surprising numbers game for you.

If you multiply ANY number from 1 on up by 9, the result will always add up to 9.

Multiply 9 times 2, you get 18. Add the 1 and 8, you get 9.
Multiply 9 times 5, you get 45. Add the 4 and 5, you get 9.
Multiply 9 times 35, you get 315. Add the 3, 1 and 5, you get 9.

A bigger example: Multiply 9 by say, 463, you get 4,167. Add the 4, 1, 6, 7, you get 18, add the 1 and 8 and there you are, 9.

Multiply 9 by any number from 1 on up and that answer always adds up to 9. Works every time.

What was ironic about the song "If I Only Had a Heart," sung by Jack Haley in the movie "The Wizard of Oz"?

Haley played the role of Tin Man in "The Wizard of Oz," and in the movie, the Tin Man wanted the Wizard to give him a heart. Haley sang the song, "If I Only Had a Heart."

Ironically, in real life, it just so happened that Haley had heart problems, and he died of a heart attack.

(If only the Wizard had really given Haley a new heart).

What was the Zero Jinx for U.S. presidents?

For 120 years, every U.S. president elected in a year ending in zero died in office.

The Zero Jinx started with William Henry Harrison, elected in 1840. Then came Abraham Lincoln elected in 1860, James Garfield in 1880, William McKinley in 1900, Warren Harding in 1920, Franklin Roosevelt in 1940 and John Kennedy in 1960. All died in office. (The way U.S. presidential elections are sequenced every four years, there were no presidential elections in 1850, 1870, 1890, 1910, 1930, 1950 and 1970).

After Kennedy in 1960, the next president elected in a zero year was Ronald Regan in 1980, and he finally beat the jinx—but just barely.

Reagan was shot coming out of a Washington hotel early in his first term, but he survived, finished his two terms, and ended the Zero Jinx.

How old are Romeo & Juliet in Shakespeare's play about them?

It might be surprising to learn that Juliet is just 13 years old in that famous love story.

Although her age is established in the play, Romeo's exact age is never mentioned, but some Shakespearean scholars believe Shakespeare implied Romeo to be around 16 or 17 years old.

How has daily dress changed in America?

Picture the scene. A woman is getting ready to go shopping. She puts on a dress—no jeans or pants—and maybe even a fine hat and stylish gloves, just to go shopping.

A man is getting ready to go to a football or baseball game. He puts on a suit and tie and no baseball cap but one of those old fedoras, just to go to a game.

That was the custom until the dress code changed in America.

It was in the decade of the 1960s that a dress code revolution hit America. It was then that people began dressing more informally at all kinds of locales like restaurants, theaters, games, businesses, stores, etc.

The nation changed in many ways in the 1960s: That was the decade of the youth rebellion, the anti-Vietnam War demonstrations, the feminist revolution, the Civil Rights movement—and the way people dress. That was a major change.

In which U.S. states do the 2 biggest cities in the state both start with the same letter?   (There are 9 such states)

In Georgia, its two biggest cities both start with "A"—Atlanta and Augusta…In Hawaii, its two biggest cities both start with "H"— Honolulu and Hilo…In Kentucky, its two biggest start with an "L"—Louisville and Lexington…In Pennsylvania, it's Philadelphia and Pittsburgh…In South Carolina, Columbia and Charleston…In

Washington, Seattle and Spokane...In Wisconsin, Milwaukee and Madison...In Wyoming, Cheyenne and Casper.

And there's one state where the three biggest cities all start with the same letter—Ohio, with Columbus, Cleveland and Cincinnati.

What was Christopher Columbus' real name? (It wasn't Columbus)

It might be surprising to know that the explorer we call Christopher Columbus never used that name in his lifetime.

He was born in Genoa, part of modern Italy, with the name Cristoforo Colombo and he went by that name for many years.

Later in his life, after going to Spain, and sailing for Spain, he changed his name to Cristobal Colon—and never went by Christopher Columbus.

Christopher Columbus is simply an English-language version of his name.

How could both teams lose the same football game?

It happened at a high school football game in Georgia in 1977.

Two Georgia teams played each other, but after the game it was discovered that both teams had used ineligible players.

The Georgia High School Football Association gave both teams a loss—and that's the way it was carried on the records—a loss for both teams.

What important item on all automobiles was invented by a woman named Mary Anderson?

Mary Anderson from Birmingham, Ala., was visiting New York City in 1903 in the early days of automobiles when she noticed drivers continually getting out of their cars to wipe rain and snow off the cars' windows.

She came up with a devise that had a rubber blade on a swinging arm that the driver could operate from inside the car—an idea she patented. She had invented the windshield wiper.

Interestingly, her windshield wipers were originally criticized as distracting to the driver, but as cars became more popular, the usefulness of Mary Anderson's windshield wipers became apparent.

Why did Congress once take 2 stripes off the U.S. flag?

Originally, a new star and a new stripe were added to the U.S. flag when a new state entered the Union. So when the 14th and 15th states—Vermont and Kentucky—joined the Union after the original 13, the flag had 15 stars and 15 stripes.

But as more states were getting ready to enter the Union, it soon dawned on members of Congress that the flag would become unwieldy if a new stripe was added for each new state.

So then Congress took away the 14th and 15th stripes and passed a law saying the flag would always stay at 13 stripes to honor the original 13 states, and only new stars would be added for new states.

What words are plural—yet don't end in "s"?

Here are some:

Men
Women
Children
Feet
Teeth
Sheep
Deer
Mice
Geese

What happened at the Metropolitan Opera to a man who sang the line, "Too bad you can only live so long"?

Opera tenor Richard Versalle was performing at the Metropolitan Opera at Lincoln Center in New York in January 1996, appearing in the opera, "The Makropulos Case." A few minutes into the first act, he sang the line, "Too bad you can only live so long."

Immediately after finishing that line, he collapsed and fell to the stage. Some in the audience might have thought that was part of the opera for him to fall to the stage, but it wasn't. Versalle had suffered a fatal heart attack right after singing that line.

The Met quickly dropped the curtain, several doctors rushed to the scene and determined Versalles had died, and the opera, in its very early moments, was cancelled. The audience was then told what had happened, and they left Lincoln Center in one of the most ironic incidents in opera history.

Why did the first person to walk on the moon—Neil Armstrong—threaten to sue his barber when he got back to Earth?

No, it wasn't because he didn't like his haircut.

Neil Armstrong who made all-time history by being the first person to walk on the moon, wanted to sue his barber because his barber, after cutting Armstrong's hair, sold some of the hair to a collector without Armstrong's prior knowledge or permission.

In the legal back-and-forth that followed, the barber was asked to give the money he made to Armstrong's favorite charity.

Who is the only U.S. president in a sports hall of fame?

The president you might think would be in a sports hall of fame is Gerald Ford who played on two national championship football teams at the University of Michigan and was voted Most Valuable Player of his team in his senior year, but Ford never made it to the college football hall of fame.

The only U.S. president who has been inducted to a sports hall of fame is… Dwight Eisenhower.

In 2009, Eisenhower was elected to the golf hall of fame for his "Love of the game and the interest he created in golf." While president, Eisenhower was known for playing a lot of golf whenever he could.

Surprisingly, how many times does the word or number one appear on the U.S. one-dollar bill?

Would you believe the word or number one appears on a U.S. one-dollar bill in 16 different places, exclusive of serial numbers?

At first glance, most people can't find all 16, but here they are.

On the front of the bill, there are four ones in figures on the four corners. The word one appears at the bottom, and on the right side in the middle of the bill. That's six ones on the front.

On the back of the bill, on the four corners, there are eight ones—four in figures and four in words, plus the word one in the middle and at the bottom of the bill. That's 10 on the back, for the total of 16.

What's the biggest thing anybody ever bought?

The record for the biggest thing ever bought goes to U.S. president Thomas Jefferson who made the Louisiana Purchase in 1803. How big was that purchase?

Jefferson bought almost a million square miles of land from France—an area that extended from the Gulf of Mexico to the Canadian border, an area extending from Louisiana to Montana.

That purchase gave the United States land that became all or parts of 15 states.

There's never been a bigger purchase than that. That's the biggest thing anybody ever bought.

What made John Philip Sousa's name a perfect name?

John Philip Sousa, who wrote "The Stars and Stripes Forever," the U.S. Marine Corps song "Semper Fidelis," and other patriotic marches had a perfect name for a famous American—and here's why:

Appropriately, his last name, Sousa, ended in USA—how perfect, and that was his real name.

It was like he was fated to be a patriotic song man. Not only that, but one more added fact about Sousa. He was born in— naturally—the nation's capital, Washington D.C.

John Philip SoUSA—Mr. USA.

What's the difference between a hurricane and a typhoon?

Despite their different names, hurricanes and typhoons are both exactly the same—with this one exception:

They're called hurricanes if they originate in the Atlantic or eastern Pacific Oceans, and they're called typhoons if they originate in the western Pacific and hit Asian coasts.

As to why hurricanes are called hurricanes, the word hurricane came to us from an old Caribbean Indian word that meant "evil wind." They got that right.

Which countries in the world have an "x" in their name, and which countries have a "z" in their name?

There are just two countries that have an "x" in their name, but surprisingly, there are 16 countries that have a "z" in their name, and here they are alphabetically:

The countries that have an "x" are Luxembourg and Mexico.

Those with a "z" are Azerbaijan, Belize, Bosnia and Herzegovina, Brazil, Czech Republic, Kazakhstan, Kyrgyzstan, Mozambique, New Zealand, Swaziland, Switzerland, Tanzania, Uzbekistan, Venezuela, Zambia and Zimbabwe.

What name did Washington, D.C. almost have?

Washington, D.C., came very close to having a different name—and if it was up to George Washington, it would have had a different name.

When the new city of Washington was being laid out as the nation's capital during George Washington's terms as president, he always referred to it—not as Washington—but as Federal City, and that's the name he said he wanted for it.

Whether it was modesty or whatever, Washington said he thought the capital should be called Federal City. So, if George Washington's idea had prevailed, we'd be saying today that the White House and Congress are in Federal City, D.C., not Washington, D.C.

Who's the only baby ever pictured on the front of U.S. money?

That baby is Jean Baptiste, but who was Jean Baptiste, and what paper money or coin was Jean Baptiste on?

Jean Baptiste was the baby son of American Indian guide Sacagawea. Sacagawea led the famous Lewis and Clark expedition to the West—and the U.S. $1 coin first minted in the year 2000, honored Sacagawea, showing her on the front of the coin carrying her baby son, Jean Baptiste.

Jean Baptiste is thus the only baby ever shown on the front of a U.S. coin or paper money.

What was the most confusing Thanksgiving the U.S. ever had?

There was a year when there were two Thanksgivings in the U.S.—and real confusion about when Thanksgiving really was.

President Franklin Roosevelt in 1939 thought it would help the economy if he advanced Thanksgiving from the fourth Thursday in November to the third Thursday to allow a longer Christmas shopping season.

Trouble was, half the states didn't accept it and kept the holiday on the fourth Thursday. The other states accepted it and celebrated it the week before.

It was confusing. If you wanted to visit grandma in another state on Thanksgiving, you had to check on which day her Thanksgiving was. Travel plans and work days nationwide were all mixed up.

Fortunately, that confusion lasted just one year and Thanksgiving went back to all on the same day the next year. Congress voted to have Thanksgiving always to be on the fourth Thursday of November every year.

What was the computer mouse originally called?

Douglas Engelbart, an early computer pioneer, is given credit as the man who invented that very useful item known as the computer mouse—except it wasn't called a mouse at the beginning.

It was originally called a "position indicator" or a "pointing devise"—but its shape, plus the wire coming out of its back, made it resemble a real mouse, and the name "mouse" it became.

No Bathrooms in the White House?

It seems hard to believe now, but in its early years there was no indoor plumbing in the White House, which was common in those days. People then used outhouses and that included presidents of the United States.

The White House opened in 1800—but it didn't get indoor plumbing until 1833, when the seventh president, Andrew Jackson, was in office.

That means the early presidents used an outhouse which was on the White House grounds.

Indoor plumbing wasn't all the White House didn't have in those days. There were no electric lights, air-conditioning, or telephones either.

Why did the U.S. government once outlaw sliced bread?

During World War II, people in the U.S. were asked to give up a lot of things to help the war effort—but why, of all things, sliced bread?

A wartime ban was put into effect in 1943 on the sale of sliced bread to reduce bakeries' need for metal replacement parts for their bread-slicing equipment. That metal was needed for war materiel.

The ban on the sale of sliced bread in the U.S. lasted until 1945.

What advice can dogs give us?

A dog-loving author once wrote some things that dogs can teach us:

Delight in the simple joy of a long walk.

When a loved one comes home, run to greet them.

Run, and play daily.

Take naps. Stretch before rising.

Be loyal.

Allow the experience of fresh air and wind in your face to be pure ecstasy.

Never pretend to be something you're not.

What's the first number that has an "a" in its name?

When you spell out all our whole numbers, starting with one, two, three, four, etc., and keep going all the way up, you would not use the letter "a" until you reach one-thousand.

Unbelievably, no whole number from one through nine-hundred-ninety-nine has an "a" in it.

Even more unbelievable, no number has a "b" until you reach one-billion. None of those first millions of whole numbers from one to one-billion has a "b" when you spell them out.

How important is football?

One of our radio listeners once sent us this classic apocryphal story that shows just how big a football game can really be.

It seems there was a big game one day, and a man we'll call Jack had two tickets on the 50-yard line to the game.

As Jack watches the game, a man behind him, Mike, notices that the seat next to Jack is empty—and has been all during the game. Mike leans over and asks Jack, "Does that empty seat next to you belong to you?" Jack answers, "Yes, it's mine, and nobody's sitting in it."

"That's incredible," said Mike. "Biggest game of the year, and the best seat in the house, right on the 50-yard line, and nobody's using that seat."

Jack answered, "The seat belongs to me. I always came with my wife. She's been coming to every game with me for years and sitting right here. But she has died. This is the first game we didn't come to together since we were married in 1970."

Mike said, "Oh, I'm sorry to hear that. That's terrible. But couldn't you find someone else—a friend, or relative, or even a neighbor, to take the seat and come to the game with you?"

"No," said Jack, shaking his head sadly. "No…they're all at the funeral."

What does "Auld Lang Syne" mean?

Many New Year's Eve revelers sing or listen to the song "Auld Lang Syne" without knowing what that phrase means.

The words were written by Scottish poet Robert Burns in 1788, and the music was from an old Scottish folk melody.

"Auld Lang Syne" means, in Scottish dialect, "Old Long Since" or, translated into modern English, "Days Gone By"—as we bid farewell to the old year.

It was popularized in America by Guy Lombardo in the 1930s when his orchestra played it on national radio every New Year's Eve. Lombardo's program was appropriately sponsored in those days by a brand of cigars known as Robert Burns cigars.

What are some predictions that went bad?

In 1977, a computer expert said "I see no reason why anyone would want a computer in their home."

An admiral speaking about the creation of the first atom bomb, said "The bomb will never go off, and I speak as an expert on explosives."

An economics professor said the stock market is sound and stocks have reached a permanent high plateau. He said that on Oct. 15, 1929. Fourteen days later, the stock market crashed and ushered in the Great Depression.

A film producer, rejecting the idea of sound coming in movies, said in 1927, "Nobody wants to hear actors talk."

Another film producer in the early days of TV said that TV would never last because, "Who wants to stare at a box all the time."

Oh well, you can't always be right.

Ever wonder why the dashboard in an automobile is called a dashboard?

The name dashboard dates back to horse-and-buggy days when dashing horses kicked up dirt and mud, splashing the passengers riding behind them.

Owners of buggies in those days put up what they called a dashboard to protect those riding in the buggies from the dirt and mud kicked up by the dashing horses.

When the first automobiles were made, that name carried over for the area in front of the driver, and the name has lasted all these years.

What was unbelievable about Gaylord Perry's home run on July 20, 1969?

It's a story that sounds too good to be true—but it is true.

The story begins in 1962 when baseball manager Alvin Dark of the San Francisco Giants was watching one of his players, pitcher Gaylord Perry, take batting practice. Dark, looking at Perry's lack of power, told some nearby sports writers, "A man will walk on the moon before Perry hits a home run in the big leagues."

Then seven years later, on July 20, 1969, Neil Armstrong became the first man to walk on the moon, and, incredibly, on that very day, Perry hit his first major league home run in a game in San Francisco. This story was verified by reporters who heard Dark's original remark and the fact that Perry did indeed hit his first home run on the day Armstrong walked on the moon.

What Halloween radio show really scared America?

On Halloween Eve 1938, actor-writer Orson Welles created a show on the CBS radio network (there was no national TV then) that opened with an orchestra playing music—BUT then quickly the music was interrupted with a news bulletin that gave an on-the-scene report of a strange object that had just landed near Grover's Mill, N.J.

The reporter said: "Ladies and gentlemen, this is the most terrifying thing I have ever seen. Creatures are crawling out. I can see the things' bodies now—they're as large as a bear. And those faces! It's so awful. They gleam like a serpent; the mouths are… kind of V-shaped, with saliva dripping from their lips that seem to quiver and pulsate."

Things happened fast from there. The announcer said soldiers were appearing on the scene. But then the announcer said heat rays from the monsters' guns were turning the soldiers into screaming flames. Suddenly the announcer was cut off the air. After a short music interlude, more bulletins began pouring in. Reports said poison gas was spreading west. Other news reporters rushed to the scene. Then one-by-one, those reporters could be heard being overcome themselves—apparently dying on the scene. One could be heard choking in an on-the-air death. Reports came of Red Cross workers arriving and being killed, and finally came the announcement from the studio that capped it…

"Ladies and gentlemen, the observations of science and the evidence we have, lead to the inescapable assumption that those strange beings who landed in the Jersey farmlands tonight are the vanguard of an invading army from the planet Mars…the monsters are now in control of the middle of New Jersey and have effectively cut the state in its center. Marshall law prevails throughout New Jersey and eastern Pennsylvania. Now reports are coming that Martian space ships are landing all over the country!"

Panic gripped America. Telephone lines were jammed. People wrapped their faces in wet towels. Hospitals were treating people for shock. A woman in Pittsburgh was ready to swallow poison until stopped by her husband. People gathered in churches to frantically pray. Rumors spread that New York City was on fire with millions of deaths. Police departments everywhere were deluged with calls.

And inside Studio One at CBS, Welles and his fellow actors went blissfully on, continuing the broadcast in complete ignorance of the havoc they were causing across the nation. The funny thing is that Welles had opened the program with a disclaimer that said this was just a fictional dramatization, but that was long forgotten as the show went on and panic spread as more people tuned in. Finally, near the end of the show, Welles nonchalantly announced that nothing had really happened, and it was all just a Halloween joke. "Ha Ha," he said, "This was our version of dressing up in a sheet and jumping out of a bush and saying boo." But he had really scared the nation.

Amazingly, almost 40% of all U.S. presidents' last names have ended in EXACTLY THE SAME LETTER. What is that letter, and who are the presidents?

All these presidents' last names have ended in the same letter—and that letter is "n."

Here they all are in the order they served—George Washington, Thomas Jefferson, James Madison, Andrew Jackson, Martin Van Buren, William Henry Harrison, James Buchanan, Abraham Lincoln, Andrew Johnson, Benjamin Harrison, Woodrow Wilson, Harry Truman, Lyndon Johnson, Richard Nixon, Ronald Reagan, Bill Clinton and Joe Biden. ALL those presidents' names end in "n"—amazing.

How long did the U.S. go without anybody having a Social Security number?

It may be surprising to learn that for more than 150 years, the United States had no Social Security. From the country's founding in 1776, all through the 1800s and into the 1900s, nobody in America got a Social Security check or had a Social Security card or Social Security number.

It was during the first term of President Franklin Roosevelt's presidency in 1935 that the U.S.'s first Social Security act was created. The act was largely written by the first woman ever chosen to be in a president's cabinet, Frances Perkins, who had been appointed secretary of labor by Roosevelt.

And the name Ida May Fuller takes a place in U.S. history. Ida May Fuller of Ludlow, Vt., became the first American to receive a monthly Social Security check. She got Social Security check No. 0001, in the princely sum of $24.54.

What sayings that we use have a food as part of the expression?

There's cool as a cucumber, spill the beans, that's the way the cookie crumbles, like two peas in a pod, flat as a pancake, couch potato, don't put all your eggs in one basket, like comparing apples and oranges, bring home the bacon, have your cake, and eat it too.

And, let's not forget in a nut shell.

Who's the youngest person ever to make a million dollars on their own?

In recent years we've seen some young people in their teens and twenties become very wealthy in the computer world, but the all-time record for being the youngest person ever to make a million dollars on their own was set by a little girl not yet 10 years old.

And this happened long before computers, back in the 1930s.

When movie star Shirley Temple was 6, 7, 8 years old in 1934-35-36, she accumulated over a million dollars from her series of hit films, and from her endorsement contracts of such things as Shirley Temple dolls and Shirley Temple dresses.

And those were 1930s dollars.

What's the strange way the bikini got its name?

It was in July, 1946, that a French fashion designer introduced a daring, skimpy, new two- piece bathing suit. But he didn't know what to call it.

While trying to decide, he noticed newspapers had stories about the United States testing a new series of nuclear bombs at a far-off small island in the Pacific Ocean named Bikini.

The French designer, wanting his new bathing suit to get media attention, and believing that his bathing suit was indeed explosive, named it after the nuclear-bomb site—Bikini, and it's been called a bikini ever since.

It's hard to imagine two more different things carrying the same name—a nuclear bomb site and a swimsuit, but that's what happened.

What was the only game in history in which EVERY starting player on one team made the baseball Hall of Fame?

At the 1934 major league baseball All-Star game, the nine players in the starting lineup for the American League ALL became members of the baseball Hall of Fame—every player in that starting lineup that day made the Hall of Fame. Fans never saw another game like that.

That starting lineup for the American League had infielders Lou Gehrig, Charlie Gehringer, Joe Cronin and Jimmy Foxx, outfielders Babe Ruth, Heine Manush and Al Simmons, catcher Bill Dickey and pitcher Lefty Gomez—all Hall of Famers.

There's never been another lineup like that, before or since.

Where is the U.S. flag never lowered to half-staff—even when a U.S. president dies or for any other person or reason?

The place where the U.S. flag is never lowered to half-staff for any reason is…the U.S. flag on the moon.

Astronauts Neil Armstrong and Buzz Aldrin left an American flag on the moon, attached at full staff to a pole and stiffened by a wire on the windless moon to give it the appearance of waving—and there it resides.

It's unable to be lowered to half-staff, at least until a human ever gets back to the moon.

There are 12 U.S. states whose names begin with a vowel. What are those 12 states?

They are Alabama, Alaska, Arizona, Arkansas, Idaho, Illinois, Indiana, Iowa, Ohio, Oklahoma, Oregon and Utah.

Why don't we use just the letter "U" when writing "you"?

Every once in a while language experts come up with ideas to simplify our spelling—eliminating unnecessary letters in words, like the U.S. did years ago when Americans shortened words like labor and color from their British spelling of labour and colour, but now a more revolutionary idea has been proposed.

In regular, formal writing, we use just the letter "I" when we write about ourselves, like, "I went shopping"—so why not use just the letter "U" by itself when we want to spell "you"?

It would save a lot of space and time. Some social networking people already do that, but do you think it will ever come in regular, formal writing?   Y not? (We could also shorten "why" to just Y).

Which U.S. presidential candidate lost support because he cried?

It happened in the 1972 presidential campaign when a leading candidate for the Democratic nomination was U.S. Senator Edmund Muskie.

During the New Hampshire primaries, a newspaper wrote some derogatory things about Muskie's wife. Muskie stood outside on a snowy day in New Hampshire and talked to the media—giving an emotional defense of his wife.

Tears began rolling down his cheeks. He later said they were really melted snowflakes, but many others thought they were tears and that Muskie had broken down and cried.

After reports that he was crying, his campaign faltered, and Muskie soon left the race.

Why is the most famous street in Washington, D.C., named after Pennsylvania and not some other state?

Many streets in Washington are named after the various U.S. states, but the most famous street is considered to be Pennsylvania Avenue because it's the street that runs from the Capitol Building to the White House.

The reason Pennsylvania Avenue was named after Pennsylvania— and not some other state—was to honor the fact that the nation's first capital city in 1776, where the Declaration of Independence was written, was Philadelphia, in Pennsylvania. It was Thomas Jefferson who suggested that Washington, D.C.'s main street be named for Pennsylvania, and so it was.

When did the first general-use credit cards appear?

It seems hard to believe, but before 1950 there were no general-use credit cards. The only credit cards available before 1950 were issued by a few gasoline companies and department stores—but those cards were good for use only at those gasoline stations or department store locations, and not usable elsewhere.

But then life changed.

In 1950, the first general-use credit card was introduced. It was called the Diners Club card which was originally honored at various restaurants, and then the idea spread, and soon other businesses and stores began accepting it.

That opened the credit card era, and Visa, MasterCard, Discover and American Express cards followed.

What famous man—a renowned world leader—started his life in a ladies' room?

That famous man who started his life in a ladies' room was the prime minister of Great Britain during World War II—a man called one of the greatest statesmen in world history—Winston Churchill.

When Churchill's mother was pregnant with Winston, she was attending a fancy party in Blenheim Palace in Britain. While at the party, she suddenly went into labor and was rushed into the nearest ladies' room.

It was there that the great Winston Churchill was born—in the ladies room.

Can you imagine the New York Stock Exchange being shut down for more than FOUR months? What event in the 20th century caused that?

It seems hard to believe now, but the New York Stock Exchange and many exchanges around the world once did shut down for over four months. It happened at the start of World War I, in the summer of 1914. The exchanges shut down from July 31 until mid-December to stop plunging stock prices.

In case you're wondering, the New York Stock Exchange shut down after the 9/11 terrorist attacks in 2001 for just four days, and there was no long shutdown during World War II. The four-and-a-half-month closing of the market in 1914 was the longest ever in the history of the stock exchange.

What's the story of why popsicles are called popsicles?

The word popsicles goes back to 1923 when a man named Frank Epperson first brought them on the market—except he didn't call them popsicles.

He originally called them an epsicle—taking three letters from his last name, "e", "p" and "s," and combining it with "icle" from the last four letters of "icicle,"to imply something cold, and thus came up with epsicle.

But the product didn't become successful. When Frank Epperson's own kids jokingly started referring to the epsicles as "pop's" icles, Frank decided to use that name—and gave the world "popsicles".

What's the longest word that doesn't have an "a," "e," "i," "o," or "u" in it?

We can start with 3-letter words like sky and try, some 4-letter words like hymn, and 5-letter words like Gypsy and lynch, but...

The longest everyday word we can think of that doesn't have an "a," "e," "i." "o," or "u" in it is a 6-letter word—rhythm.

You can even make it a 7-letter word without an 'a,' 'e,' "i,' "o," or "u" by making it plural—rhythms.

When did an airplane crash into the Empire State Building—and what happened?

It's little-remembered today, but in 1945, a U.S. Army plane got lost in the fog over New York City and slammed into the 79th floor of the Empire State Building.

Fuel on the plane exploded and flames engulfed four floors. The plane created a hole 18 feet wide and 20 feet high in the building.

Fortunately, it was a Saturday and most offices were vacant, but 14 people were killed—11 office workers who happened to be there, and the plane's crew of three.

Impressively, the Empire State Building withstood the hit. Outside of damage to four floors, there were no major structural problems—and the building opened for business the following Monday morning.

What was true of U.S. Congressmen Robert Cornell and Robert Drinan that was not true of any other U.S. Congressman in history?

U.S. House of Representative members Robert Cornell and Robert Drinan were both Catholic priests.

Father Cornell was elected to the U.S. House of Representatives from Wisconsin and served from 1975 to 1979. Father Drinan was elected to the U.S. House from Massachusetts and served from 1971 to 1981.

They remain the only Catholic priests ever elected to Congress.

How surprisingly long did it take for automobiles to get seat belts?

For the first 50 years or so of automobiles, they didn't have seat belts.

The first seat belts in cars didn't appear until after World War II, in the late 1940s —and then they were just an optional feature. They began to become standard in some cars by the late 1950s but there were no laws requiring their use.

The world's first seat belt law for cars was enacted in 1970 in the state of Victoria in Australia, making the wearing of seat belts mandatory for drivers and front-seat passengers. It took a while after that for U.S. states to begin passing seat belt laws and for much of the driving public to begin using seat belts on a regular basis.

An interesting fact about seat belts is that long before they were used in cars, they were used in airplanes with a different name. They were originally called safety belts in airplanes, but a public relations advisor to the airlines suggested that name implied questions about airline safety, so the name was changed from safety belts to seat belts.

If there are aliens out there on some far-off planets, what would they look like?

Several scientists have recently come up with some theories. Would aliens be little green men and women? Well, as one scientist says, they may well have different skin colors, but even we have that.

He and others feel aliens would probably look much like us because our bodies are efficient for building things—with two arms and hands, although one scientist speculated they may have as many as six appendages with some combination of six arms and legs like our insects do.

Another scientist says aliens probably would have heads like ours because our heads are efficient for holding brains, eyes and mouth, although aliens might have more than two eyes.

Come to think of it, an eye in the back of the head could be valuable.

How did the president of Russia get a Super Bowl ring?

The owner of the New England Patriots, Robert Kraft, made a business trip to Russia a few years after the Patriots had won the Super Bowl and was wearing his Super Bowl ring.

At a meeting with Russian president Vladimir Putin, Putin admired the ring and Kraft took it off to give Putin a better look.

Putin then put it in his pocket and kept it. Some say Kraft intended to give it to Putin as a gift, but others say Kraft was just showing it to Putin—and when Putin kept it, to be nice or for business reasons, Kraft let him keep it.

In any case, Russian leader Vladimir Putin got a Super Bowl ring.

What was wrong with the name Pony Express?

The Pony Express was a famous chapter in American history, carrying the mail from the Midwest to the Pacific Coast.

But there are a couple of surprises about it.

Despite its name, the Pony Express didn't use ponies. It was called the Pony Express, but they used full-sized horses—and not ponies. So, no ponies were used in the Pony Express.

And it had a surprisingly short life. For all its fame, it lasted just 19 months, from April 1860 to October 1861.

It had a glamorous aura, but was a financial failure and lost over $200,000 in its short run.

What mistakes have been made in movies?

Here are some memorable ones:

In "Ben Hur," during the film's famous chariot race, you can see a red automobile in the distance. They didn't have automobiles then. The film takes place in A.D. 26.

In the classic movie, "Casablanca," Humphrey Bogart is leaving Paris by train, and his coat gets sopping wet from rain while he's waiting outside the train for Ingrid Bergman. A moment later, he steps on the train, and his coat is suddenly completely dry.

In "Million Dollar Baby," Hillary Swank is driving in what's supposed to be Missouri where she just bought a home for her mother. But why are there palm trees on the side of the road—in Missouri?

In the famous Battle of Atlanta scene in "Gone With the Wind," Vivien Leigh runs by an electric street light. Unfortunately, electric lights didn't exist during the Civil War.

John Travolta is told in "Face/Off" that a bomb will go off in six days. The bomb shows the time left before it goes off. It reads 216 hours. That's nine days.

In the 1994 film "Forrest Gump," there's a scene that's supposed to be taking place around 1970—but a person in the scene is reading a USA Today newspaper. USA Today didn't start publishing until 1982.

What major scientific event happened at a football stadium?

The University of Chicago had given up football in the 1940s, and had no games scheduled during the 1942 season, making their stadium, and the space under the stands, available for top-secret experiments.

On Dec. 2, 1942, scientists, working under the stands at the University of Chicago's football stadium, created the first controlled nuclear chain reaction—and at that instant, the nuclear age was born.

And so, one of history's biggest scientific milestones occurred, of all places, at a football stadium.

Which 7 U.S. presidents had a different name when they were born than when they were president?

Bill Clinton was born Bill Blythe. After his father's death, his mother later married a man named Clinton, and as a teenager, Bill Blythe took his stepfather's last name and became Bill Clinton.

Gerald Ford was born Leslie King. His parents divorced and his mother later married a man named Gerald Ford. Young Leslie King took his stepfather's first and last name and became Gerald Ford Jr.

Dwight Eisenhower was born David Dwight Eisenhower but later switched his first and middle names.

Calvin Coolidge, Woodrow Wilson, Grover Cleveland and Ulysses Grant all dropped their first names completely. Coolidge was born John Calvin Coolidge, Wilson was Thomas Woodrow Wilson, Cleveland was Stephen Grover Cleveland, and Grant was Hiram Ulysses Grant.

If animals could play cards, which animals would you not want to play with?

We got many creative answers to this question from listeners on our radio show, and here are some:

You would not want to play cards with:

A shark because he might be a card shark. A giraffe because he could look over your hand. A rabbit because he'd bring a rabbit's foot for his luck. A boar because he'd be boring. A cheetah because he's a cheetah (cheater). A laughing hyena because he'd laugh at you. A crab because he'd be unpleasant. Elks, moose and lions because they have all the clubs. A seeing-eye dog because he might see through your cards. A pregnant cat because she'd take the kitty.

Why do people fold their hands while saying a prayer?

The custom of people folding their hands while praying began when teachers and clergymen taught children to fold their hands in prayer to keep their hands from doing anything else that would be distracting while praying, and to help keep their attention on the prayer. The custom then spread to adults as well.

Folding hands in prayer eventually became a tradition in many religions.

What are the 8 Ivy League colleges—and what's the only state that has 2 of them?

The eight Ivy League colleges, in alphabetical order, are Brown, Columbia, Cornell, Dartmouth, Harvard, Pennsylvania, Princeton and Yale.

The only state that has two Ivy League colleges is New York, with Columbia in New York City and Cornell in Ithaca, N.Y.

Which U.S. senator has had the perfect name to be president?

If ever a person had the right name to be president of the United States, it's a man who was first elected to the U.S. Senate in 2006.

That man with the perfect name to be president has been a senator from Rhode Island. His name: Sheldon Whitehouse.

Just think: If Sheldon Whitehouse ever became president, news reports would be saying: "At the White House today, President Whitehouse said such and such."

In case you're wondering, Sheldon Whitehouse is his real name.

Why is Valentine's Day named after St. Valentine?

There was a bishop in Rome in the third century whose name really was Valentine, but Valentine defied the emperor.

Valentine performed marriages of young soldiers and their girlfriends even though the emperor had banned soldiers from getting married because, he said, marriage made poor-quality soldiers.

For defying the emperor, Valentine was beheaded—on February 14, in the year 269.

But love triumphed after all. Two hundred years later, the pope honored Valentine, and declared February 14, in the year 496, as the first Valentine's Day in memory of St. Valentine.

There's more to the story. When Valentine was in prison, awaiting his execution, a blind girl came to him. He miraculously restored her sight and left a farewell message that read: "From your Valentine"—a phrase that would live on.

When did nations of the world actually outlaw war?

There was once a momentous treaty signed by most nations of the world—but, boy, did it not work.

In 1928, most major nations signed what was known as the Kellogg-Briand Peace Treaty, named after the U.S. secretary of state, Frank Kellogg, and the French foreign minister, Aristide Briand.

That treaty outlawed war—saying nations would never start another war again.

Many people rejoiced then—no more wars, they said. It was a big deal when signed, but is pretty much forgotten today.

Needless to say, the Kellogg-Briand Peace Treaty did not work.

What words are pronounced exactly like another word, yet spelled differently?

Ah, the oddities of the English language. Ever realize how many words are pronounced exactly the same—but spelled differently.

You can have some fun thinking of many yourself, but here are a few to get started. How about "night" and "knight." Or "Mary" and "merry." Or "isle" and "aisle." "To", "too" and "two" are all pronounced the same.

And one of the craziest of all: There's "you," and a female sheep which is called a "ewe". They're pronounced the same but have NO letters in common. Same with "I" and "eye."

English can be a funny language.

Which U.S. vice president ran a tavern and was a nightly bartender—while he was vice president?

It happened when Richard Johnson was vice president under President Martin Van Buren from 1837 to 1841. The salary for U.S. vice presidents in those days was —would you believe—only $5,000 a year, and VP Johnson wanted to supplement his income.

So he opened and ran a tavern —serving drinks while serving as the nation's vice president.

No one apparently seemed to mind. The media didn't pay much attention to it and Johnson was popular on Capitol Hill, having been a congressman before becoming VP.

Incidentally, that $5,000 salary for vice presidents was in effect from 1789 until 1873 when it was raised to...$10,000 a year. It's now over $200,000.

How did Rudolph the Red-Nosed Reindeer come to be?

The words to "Rudolph the Red-Nosed Reindeer" were originally written—not as a song—but as a newspaper ad and advertising handout for the Montgomery-Ward department store in Chicago at Christmastime in 1939. The words were written by advertising man Robert May.

Eight years later, in 1947, May's brother-in-law, songwriter Johnny Marks, wrote music to those words, and tried to get someone to record it. Nobody would.

Finally, Gene Autry, as a favor to Marks, put it on the flipside of a record he was doing—and to everybody's surprise, Rudolph became one of the biggest hits in music history.

One more note: May was originally going to call his reindeer "Rollo," but his 4-year-old daughter suggested "Rudolph"—and Rudolph became the most famous reindeer of all.

Why is New York's Times Square called Times Square?

That name has nothing to do with watching the time there as the ball drops on New Year's Eve. No, Times Square got its name for another reason.

Times Square was originally called Longacre Square, but in 1904 the New York Times newspaper made a deal with the city of New York.

They said they'd move to a new building there if the city would agree to change the name of the square, and name it after the New York Times.

The city agreed, and Times Square it became.

What popular song did Sue Hicks inspire?

Sue Hicks was a lawyer and later a judge in Tennessee who

inspired the Grammy Award-winning song, "A Boy Named Sue," for, you see, Sue Hicks was a male.

He was named Sue after his mother who died a few days after giving birth to him.

Sue Hicks was one of the prosecutors in the 1925 Scopes evolution trial, and then had a long career as a judge in Tennessee, stretching into the 1970s.

Songwriter Shel Silverstein heard Hicks speak at a conference one day and got the idea for the "A Boy Named Sue" song.

Johnny Cash recorded it in 1969, and after it became a big hit, Cash sent an autographed picture to Sue Hicks with the inscription, "To Sue, how do you do."

How did Alexander Graham Bell think we should answer the phone?

Alexander Graham Bell is credited with a great invention—the telephone—but he didn't have such a great idea on how it should be answered.

Bell thought people should answer the phone by saying, "ahoy." Bell thought ahoy was the proper way to answer the phone, and at first, people did say ahoy when answering the phone.

It was Thomas Edison and some others who campaigned for using "hello" as the telephone greeting and gradually, hello replaced ahoy.

We might add though that there was a church in recent years that instructed its staff to answer the phone by saying "heck-o" instead of "hell-o." But heck-o apparently has not caught on.

What made the Yreka Bakery in Yreka, Calif., so unusual?

Yreka is a small town of about 7,000 population in northern California, and for many years there was a bakery there named the Yreka Bakery. What's the big deal about that?

Yreka Bakery became famous for having its name—Yreka Bakery—spelled the same backward or forward.

Which U.S. state got its name to pay off a debt?

When Pennsylvania was still a British colony before the Revolutionary War, it was originally named Sylvania, which is Latin for "beautiful woods".

But King Charles II of England owed money to Sylvania's developer, William Penn, and instead of giving Penn any money to pay off the debt, the king gave Penn an honor by adding Penn's name to Sylvania—naming it, Penn-sylvania.

To this day we don't know whether Penn would rather have had the money or the honor, but he did get a state named after him forevermore.

What is "The Curse of 27"?

The fact that an amazing number of popular musicians died exactly at age 27 has given rise to what is known as "The Curse of 27."

By last count, 44 popular musicians have died at that age, including such stars as Jimi Hendrix, Janis Joplin, Jim Morrison, Kurt Cobain and Amy Winehouse.

In 2008, Winehouse, then 24 years old, wrote that she feared dying at 27, and as fate would have it, she did die at age 27, in 2011.

The song, "28," by John Craigie is about the "Curse," and those who didn't make it to age 28.

What are the most points scored by one team in a college football game?

There's never been a college football game like this one.

Georgia Tech beat Cumberland College in a game in 1916 by the score of 222-0 to set the all-time record.

The coach of Georgia Tech then was the famous John Heisman for whom the Heisman Trophy is named. It seems Heisman had a feud with Cumberland and rolled up the score on them in record-setting proportions.

What's strange on U.S. coins about the words penny, nickel, dime and quarter?

Just about everybody calls the 1-cent coin a penny, but the word penny doesn't appear anywhere on U.S. 1-cent coins. Likewise just about everybody calls the 5-cent coin a nickel, yet the word nickel doesn't appear anywhere there, BUT...

On the other hand, people call the 10-cent coin a dime and that word dime IS on that coin, and most people call the 25-cent coin a quarter and that word quarter is on that coin.

So why don't they put the word penny on the penny and the word nickel on the nickel? The Mint has no answer for that. Just tradition, they say.

What are the 5 largest states in the U.S. in size—and what are the 5 smallest?

Interestingly, all five of the biggest states in land area in the United States are west of the Mississippi, and four of the five smallest states are all east of the Mississippi.

The five biggest U.S. states are, in order, Alaska, Texas, California, Montana and New Mexico.

The five smallest in order are Rhode Island, Delaware, Connecticut, Hawaii and New Jersey. Of those five smallest, only Hawaii is west of the Mississippi.

Which U.S. president weighed less than 100 pounds—while he was president?

This lightest of all US presidents was James Madison who was also the shortest president.

Madison was just 5 feet, 4 inches tall to go along with his less than 100 pound weight.

Despite the fact that Madison was considered frail, he, oddly enough, was the only U.S. president to actively lead troops in battle while he was president. He led troops in fighting the British when the British invaded Washington during the War of 1812.

And this smallest of all U.S. presidents did some big work on the U.S. Constitution. He was given the name of The Father of the Constitution for his contributions to the writing of the Constitution.

Which U.S. ship disaster had a higher death toll than the Titanic?

We all know about the Titanic, but surprisingly, there was a worse ship disaster in the United States that hardly anyone seems to talk about or know about, yet it had a bigger loss of life than the Titanic.

The S.S. Sultana, a Mississippi River steam boat, was bringing soldiers home from the South after the Civil War in 1865. Steaming up the Mississippi, a boiler on the Sultana exploded, turning the ship into a raging inferno, killing almost everyone on board.

The official death count was 1,547—making it the worst ship disaster in U.S. history. The official death toll on the Titanic was 1,514, so the Sultana disaster had a higher death toll, yet we always hear about the Titanic but hardly ever, if ever, about the Sultana. We wonder why.

In baseball, how could a batter who failed to hit in 7,245 at bats be considered the greatest hitter of all time?

Incredibly, a man who, as a batter, made 7,245 outs in major league baseball turned out to be the greatest hitter in baseball history.

That man was Ty Cobb who batted 11,434 times in the majors, and made 7,245 outs, but he made 4,189 hits in those 11,434 at bats, and that gave him a lifetime batting average of .366—and that's the highest lifetime batting average in major league history.

So Ty Cobb proves you can fail many times and still be great.

Who was the one-eyed president of the U.S.?

Theodore Roosevelt, U.S. president in the early 1900s, was one of the most energetic presidents, practicing what he called the strenuous life, enjoying hiking, swimming, horseback riding, hunting and boxing.

One evening while he was president, he had a friendly boxing match with a naval aide.

The naval aide landed a blow on Roosevelt's right eye which unfortunately detached the retina in the eye. Roosevelt lost sight in that eye the rest of his life—and became the only one-eyed U.S. president in history.

Why is the Pentagon called the Pentagon?

The word "pentagon" means five-sided, and the famous building known as the Pentagon takes its name from its shape with its five sides and five concentric rings.

And although it's only five stories high, it is one of the biggest office buildings in the world with office space for as many as 30,000 people. It is a sprawling building with a total of over 17 miles of corridors in its five rings.

The Pentagon was built in the early 1940s, during World War II, to hold the burgeoning Department of Defense.

Where is it Christmas every day?

There's an island in the Indian Ocean, a possession of Australia, whose name is Christmas Island. It got that name because it had been discovered on a Christmas day.

There's also an island known as Christmas Island in the Pacific Ocean, part of the country of Kiribati that was discovered on Christmas Eve years ago.

And, in Nova Scotia, Canada, there's a Christmas Island. It got its name from an early resident there whose last name was Christmas.

So, on those three Christmas islands in the world, you could say it's Christmas every day.

Why are Ferris wheels called Ferris wheels?

Ferris wheels were invented by, and named after, a man with four names—George Washington Gale Ferris, but Ferris gave only his last name to Ferris wheels.

Ferris was an American engineer, specializing in bridge construction, and in 1893, he built the world's first Ferris wheel for the Chicago World's Fair. That first Ferris wheel was one of the biggest ever, 250 feet high and able to carry 260 people.

Although Ferris wheels then began to be used around the world, unfortunately, Ferris himself couldn't enjoy his invention much longer. He died just three years later, at age 37.

Why was it appropriate that Buzz Aldrin walked on the moon?

Perhaps it was fate that made Buzz Aldrin one of the first men to walk on the moon.

It turns out that Aldrin's mother's maiden name was, of all things… Moon.

His mother was Marion Moon.

Amazingly, the brother of a man who killed a U.S. president is in the Hall of Fame for Great Americans. Who is that man?

Edwin Booth, was a respected, leading actor of the American theater in the mid-1800s, and was elected to the Hall of Fame for Great Americans which honors great Americans in many fields.

But, it was Edwin Booth's brother, John Wilkes Booth, who was the man who shot and killed President Abraham Lincoln.

Why is it called badminton (why not goodminton)?

Ever wonder how the game of badminton got that name?

A game similar to badminton was originally played in India and called Poona. British army officers stationed there in the 1800s played the game and liked it, changed the rules a bit, and brought it back to England.

In England, the Duke of Beaufort set up courts for the game to be played at his estate. The duke's estate was named Badminton. The game took its name from his estate—and badminton it became.

What's the tallest structure ever built in the U.S.?

Surprisingly, the tallest structure ever built in the United States is not in any big city, but in a little town in North Dakota.

The tallest man-made structure in the U.S. is a TV tower in Blanchard, N.D., near the North Dakota-Minnesota border. That tower is 2,063 feet high—higher than any of the tallest buildings in the U.S.

In fact, that North Dakota TV tower has been for years the tallest man-made structure anywhere in the Western Hemisphere.

What's the world's deadliest animal—the animal that kills the most people each year?

The world's deadliest animal is not some big ferocious animal, but the little, lowly mosquito.

The World Health Organization estimates that mosquitos kill more than 2 million people every year by transmitting some of the most harmful human diseases, particularly in places like Africa and Central and South America.

Mosquitos transmit such diseases as yellow fever, malaria and various viruses, causing authorities to say that, based on the deaths they cause in many parts of the world, those little mosquitos are the world's deadliest animals.

(For those who may wonder if mosquitos should be called animals, mosquitos are insects and scientists classify insects as animals).

The city of Walla Walla, Wash. (population 31,000) is one of the places in the world that have the same word twice in their name—what others are there?

There's Pago Pago in American Samoa, Baden-Baden in Germany, Wagga Wagga in Australia, Paw Paw in Michigan, Dum Dum in India, and Bora Bora in French Polynesia.

A city slogan in Walla Walla, Wash., is that "the town is so nice, they named it twice." (Actually, the name Walla Walla comes from an American Indian term meaning "place of many waters").

Why are traffic lights red, green and yellow?
Why those colors? Why not, say, blue?

The custom of using red for stop and green for go originated with railroads in the 1800s, before automobiles or electric lights.

Railway men used red and green gas lamps and flags for signaling trains. Red was picked for stop because it's an ancient symbol for danger while green was chosen because it's considered a calming color and a good choice to proceed. Yellow was chosen for caution because it contrasts well with red and green.

When automobiles came along, it naturally followed to use the railroad custom of red, green and yellow. The first electric traffic lights were installed in Cleveland in the early 1900s where they had an added feature—a buzzer sounded every time the light changed. Not a bad idea.

What father and son combination hit homers together in the same big league baseball game?

It's unlikely we'll ever see the likes of this again.

On Sept. 14, 1990, Ken Griffey Sr. and Ken Griffey Jr.—father and son—not only appeared in the same big league baseball game together, but they batted back-to-back, one following the other in the batting order, and in the first inning of a game that night against the California Angels, they each hit a home run, back to back.

Three unique things—a father and his son both playing in the same big league baseball game; they were in the lineup back-to-back; and they each hit home runs back-to-back in the same inning. Nothing like that had ever happened in major league baseball.

How did the Wizard of Oz get that name of Oz?

Frank Baum, who wrote "The Wizard of Oz," chose the name of the wizard this way:

While writing "The Wizard of Oz," Baum took a break one day and was gazing around his office trying to decide what to call the wizard. Baum saw the letters on his three file drawers across the room. One file read "A-G," the next "H-N," and the third "O-Z."

"Hmm," Baum said. "OZ. Not bad for a name."

And "Oz" it became.

What's the name of that country—is it the Netherlands or Holland?

People often refer to the Netherlands as Holland, but Holland is really only part of the Netherlands. Holland—divided into North Holland and South Holland—makes up just two of the 12 provinces of the Netherlands.

But, oddly, the whole country of the Netherlands is often called Holland after just those two provinces.

Then, there's that word "Dutch." Dutch is the name of the language of the Netherlands, and people from the Netherlands or Holland are often called Dutch.

Which U.S. president suffered the most embarrassing defeat when he ran for a second term?

William Howard Taft had been elected president in 1908, but when he ran for a second term in 1912, he not only lost, but didn't even finish second. He finished third in a three-way race and carried only two states —Vermont and Utah.

Opposing Taft in that election were Woodrow Wilson and Theodore Roosevelt. Roosevelt had been president before but was trying for a comeback. Wilson won the election with a whopping 435 Electoral College votes. Third-party candidate Roosevelt got 88 Electoral College votes, and poor President Taft got only eight—the worst defeat ever for an incumbent president running for re-election.

How did the Tonys and the Emmys get those names?

The theater awards, the Tonys, are named after Antoinette Perry whose nickname was Tony, and who was an actress, director, a founder of the American Theater Wing and active in promoting theater. The awards were named in her honor after her death in 1946.

The TV awards—the Emmys—were named after a tube that made TV possible. It was the image orthicon tube that was originally called an "immy" by TV people in the early days of television. When the TV awards statue was created in 1948, it was a feminine figure, so organizers feminized the name "immy" and called it "Emmy."

Why don't you ever want to visit the planet Venus?

Venus has an almost unbelievable climate.

Hot, hurricane-force winds constantly circle Venus. Its surface temperatures hover around 850 degrees Fahrenheit. Venus has a constant cloud cover that keeps the heat in.

Not only is it incredibly hot on Venus, with searing winds, but there's also lightning frequently flashing above the surface, and sulfuric acid raining down.

If ever a place fit a description of Hell, Venus is it.

Ironically, despite its hellish atmosphere, Venus looks so peaceful and pretty from afar. It was named Venus after the Roman goddess of love and beauty—but it's not very pretty on its surface and in its atmosphere.

What was extremely unusual about the book "Gadsby"?

In 1939, Ernest Wright wrote a book called "Gadsby" (not to be confused with F. Scott Fitzgerald's "Great Gatsby." That was another book). In Ernest Wright's "Gadsby," there is this amazing feature:

It's a novel of over 50,000 words, and not one of those words has the letter "e" in it.

"E" is the most-used letter in the alphabet, but Wright took a challenge and wrote a coherent story of over 50,000 words without using any word that has an "e". To help, he tied down the "e" key on his typewriter so he wouldn't use an "e" by mistake.

To realize how hard this is, try writing just a few paragraphs about anything without using an "e". Ernest Wright did it in his over 50,000- word book. And he even used some long words like hospitalization and philosophically.

What was appropriate about the name of the person who invented the cheeseburger?

The person given credit by many food historians as the creator of the cheeseburger, appropriately, had a good last name as the developer of the world's first cheeseburger.

It was in 1926 that, as a teenager, working in his father's sandwich shop in Pasadena, Calif., Lionel Sternberger got the idea one evening to put a piece of cheese on a hamburger—and created the world's first cheeseburger.

The fact that his last name ended in berger turned out to be a good name for the inventor of the cheeseburger.

Which woman married the presidents of TWO different countries?

The woman who holds this unusual record was Graca Mandela.

She married Nelson Mandela when he was president of South Africa in 1998, and she became the first lady of South Africa.

Previous to that, she was first lady of another country, Mozambique. She was the wife of Samora Machel when he was president of Mozambique in the 1970s and 80s. He was killed in a plane crash in 1986 and 12 years later Graca married President Mandela of South Africa to become the only woman ever to be first lady of two separate countries.

How long did it take air conditioning to come to homes in America?

It may seem hard to believe now, but virtually no home in America had air conditioning any time before World War II.

Air conditioning was invented in the early 1900s, but not for the purpose of cooling homes.

Air conditioning was originally developed by a man named Willis Carrier to control humidity in printing plants so paper would not expand or contract while going through printing presses.

Only later, beginning in the 1920s, did air conditioning come to some stores and then to theaters, but it didn't generally begin to come to offices, automobiles and homes until the late 1940s.

There were a lot of sweltering days in homes, offices and cars before that.

Which U.S. vice president was indicted for murder?

When Aaron Burr was vice president of the United States under Thomas Jefferson in 1804, he had disputes with his political rival Alexander Hamilton, and challenged Hamilton to a gun duel.

Burr shot and killed Hamilton in that duel, and Burr was indicted for murder.

He left New Jersey where the duel was fought, never returned, and, amazingly, continued to serve as vice president of the United States while under indictment for murder, completing his vice presidential term in 1805.

Burr never was brought to trial on that indictment but was arrested in 1807 and charged with treason for allegedly attempting to form a republic in the Southwest. He was acquitted on that charge and resumed his law practice in New York until his death in 1836.

Why is the 22nd U.S. president buried in the same grave as the 24th U.S. president?

How could it be—the 22nd U.S. president and the 24th U.S. president are buried in the same grave, in Princeton, N.J.?

Yes, the 22nd and 24th presidents are buried in the same grave because...the 22nd and 24th president are really the same person—Grover Cleveland.

Cleveland was elected the 22nd U.S. president in 1884. Then he ran for a second term in 1888 but was defeated by the man who became the 23rd president, Benjamin Harrison.

Cleveland came back to run again in 1892, and won, being elected as the 24th president. According to a government ruling, he is officially counted as both the 22nd and 24th president because his two terms were not consecutive. He is the only president to serve non-consecutive terms.

It's surprising how many capital cities of countries in Europe all start with the letter "B." Which are those capital cities of European countries whose names start with "B"?

There's Brussels, Belgium; Berlin, Germany; Budapest, Hungary; Belfast, Northern Ireland; Bucharest, Romania; Belgrade, Serbia; Bratislava, Slovakia; and Bern, Switzerland.

In what order are ingredients listed on food packages?

Before we get to the answer to this question, there's the story about a customer who wrote to a food manufacturer asking what ingredients were in a package of food she had just bought. This was in the days before companies were required to list ingredients on their packages.

The manufacturer wrote back, "It's against our policy to disclose what ingredients we use." Such policy was not unusual in the old days when some manufacturers wanted to keep their ingredients a secret either for competitive reasons, or unscrupulous ones, or both.

Now, of course, by law, they have to list ingredients on packages. Listed first is what there's the most of, then the other ingredients are listed in descending order of quantity.

Why is the U.S. national election day in November—why November?

The reason Election Day is in November is because when Congress originally set the month for elections in the early years of the nation, the majority of people lived on farms or in rural areas.

By November, the harvest was in, and the many dirt roads then were not yet impassable because of winter weather. December, January and February were ruled out because of possible bad weather in the North. March through August were ruled out because farmers were busy planting then or tending to crops, and in September-October they were bringing in the harvest.

So November was the logical month, and November it has been all these years.

What was the biggest celebration ever held in America?

The biggest, wildest, most incredible celebration in American history happened on the night of August. 14, 1945.

News announcer Bob Trout of CBS went on the air on all networks on that evening at 7 p.m. Eastern time, and made the announcement that Japan had just surrendered, and World War II was over.

Celebrations erupted across America.

The biggest war the world had ever seen was over and the nation-wide celebrations in America that August night were like those never seen before or since.

In cities and towns throughout the nation, millions of people rushed into the streets, shouting with joy. Horns honked. People hugged total strangers. Happy, loud noise was heard everywhere.

To show the extent of feeling in the country, the staid New York Times the next morning had a headline that read "END OF WAR!"—using a rare exclamation point in their headline. Speaking of New York, police estimated that more than 2-million people jammed Times Square that evening to celebrate, with, as the Times said, "A din that was overwhelming." Life magazine, then the big circulation, influential weekly national publication, printed the still-famous picture of a male sailor at Times Square grabbing a female nurse who he didn't know and planting a big kiss on her. In normal times, he might have at least gotten a slap in the face for that, but not that night.

How giddy was President Truman that night? He quickly announced there would be a TWO-DAY federal holiday, starting the next day, with no mail delivery, no federal offices open, so everybody could forget about work—and celebrate. Private businesses took their cue from Truman and most offices were closed to allow everyone a gleeful two-day holiday.

There have been big celebrations in various cities and towns after a local team won a sports championship, but the difference here was that this celebration was not confined to one locale. It was nation-wide and it was the most gigantic celebration ever seen throughout the country.

Where is Timbuktu?

You've probably heard the word "Timbuktu"—as an expression for a far off place. Well, there really is a Timbuktu.

Timbuktu is an actual town in the country of Mali in western Africa. At one time, in its golden age from the 12th to the 16th centuries, it was a famous city. Timbuktu was a major center of trade and learning.

But then Timbuktu and its country, Mali, fell on hard times as a result of shifting trade routes and invasions by different tribes. Today, the once-thriving Timbuktu is a minor, impoverished, small town, nothing like it once was.

Which 2 positions in the president's cabinet are really misnamed?

Take the Secretary of the Interior. Why that name? The Secretary of the Interior is in charge of things OUTDOORS, like national parks, government-owned land, the bureau of fish and wildlife, and water supplies. Perhaps the secretary should be called Secretary of the Exterior.

And, then there's the Secretary of State. The Secretary of State does not oversee U.S. states, but is concerned strictly with foreign affairs. The Secretary of State, in fact, was originally called Secretary of Foreign Affairs, but the name was changed in 1789.

Maybe they should go back to that old name, Secretary of Foreign Affairs.

Of all the newspaper articles ever published, which one has been reprinted the most times?

It's the famous answer to the letter 8-year-old Virginia O'Hanlon wrote to the New York Sun newspaper in 1897 asking, "Is there really a Santa Claus?"

The editor, Francis Church, responded with one of the classic editorials in newspaper history, saying, "Yes, Virginia, there is a Santa Claus...He exists as certainly as love and generosity and devotion exist...Thank God he lives, and will continue to make glad the heart of childhood."

Many newspapers still reprint that every year, and they've been doing it for over 100 years.

And what of that little girl, Virginia O'Hanlon, who started it all? She lived to age 81. She died in 1971 after working as a teacher in the New York City public school system for 47 years.

There are 12 teams in the 4 major pro sports leagues that have the name of a color in their nickname. Which teams are those?

In major league baseball, there are the Boston Red Sox, Chicago White Sox, Cincinnati Reds, St. Louis Cardinals and Toronto Blue Jays.

In the National Football League, there are the Arizona Cardinals and Cleveland Browns.

In the National Hockey League, there are the Chicago Blackhawks, Columbus Blue Jackets, Detroit Red Wings, St. Louis Blues and Vegas Golden Knights.

In the National Basketball Association, oddly enough, there are none.

What's the only letter in the alphabet not used in the name of any U.S. state?

A person trying to answer this question might think first of the letter "x" or "z", but those letters are found in the name of a U.S. state. There's an "x" in Texas and a "z" in Arizona.

The only letter not used in the name of any U.S. state is "q".

What man actually bought a nation and named it after himself?

The wealthy Johann von Liechtenstein bought an area in Europe between Switzerland and Austria in 1712—an area previously called Vaduz and Schellenberg—and with his purchase, created the country of Liechtenstein.

That country of Liechtenstein still exists today. It's small, with a population of just over 30,000, but it's a strong financial center. It's an independent nation, a member of the U.N.—and still named after the man who went out and bought it, Johann von Liechtenstein.

What did the first microwave ovens look like?

When microwave ovens first came out after World War II, they were as big as refrigerators, weighed more than 700 pounds and cost several thousand dollars. And, those first microwaves weren't even made for homes, but for restaurants.

The first home microwave ovens began appearing in American kitchens in the mid-1950s and they were still rather bulky and very expensive. But gradually manufacturers learned how to reduce their size, and cost.

Ultimately, those former giant microwaves for restaurants got much smaller and began a revolution in the way people prepare everyday food at home.

When was the last year with all even numbers and no odd numbers or zeros?

The year 888—that was over a thousand years ago—was the last year that had all even numbers, and no odd numbers or zeros. And it will be a long time until there's another year with all even numbers and no odd numbers or zeros.

It can't happen in this century because all years have a zero in them, like 2016. And in the next century all years will have an odd number, the number one, as in 2116.

The next time there will be a year with all even numbers and no odd numbers or zeros will be the year 2222.

That seems hard to believe, but it's true. All past years since 888 have had an odd number and/or a zero, and all current and future years until 2222 will also have an odd number and/or a zero.

Which U.S. president had the most children—and had so many, he ran out of names?

Although John Tyler was far from being one of the most famous U.S. presidents, he did set an all-time record among presidents.

Tyler fathered 15 children.

With his first wife, Letitia, he had eight children, including ones named Robert and John. Then when Tyler was president in 1842, his wife died and two years later at age 54, he married 24-year-old Julia Gardiner. They had seven children together—the last when he was 70, by the way—and they named two of their kids Robert and John.

Tyler's first Robert and John were still living when his second Robert and John were born, so there might have been some confusion in the family when Tyler spoke of his sons Robert and John.

Why is the Red Cross called the Red Cross?

When the Red Cross was created in the 1800s, its organizers wanted a name and symbol that would honor its founder, Jean-Henri Dunant of Switzerland.

The flag of Dunant's native country of Switzerland is a white cross on a red background, They couldn't use the exact flag of Switzerland, so they reversed the colors of the Swiss flag, and came up with their symbol and their name—a red cross on a white background—and thus, the Red Cross.

Dunant got the idea for an organization like the Red Cross when he witnessed a wartime battle in 1859 and was shocked at the lack of care given to the wounded soldiers and civilians.

For his efforts in the creation of the Red Cross, Dunant won the first Nobel Peace Prize, but after founding the Red Cross, his own life became sad. He went bankrupt, and for 15 years his whereabouts were unknown. He was eventually found living in poverty.

What was the first national park in America?

Yellowstone was not only the first national park in the United States, but it was also the first park ever designated a national park anywhere in the world. By an act of Congress, Yellowstone was made the first national park in 1872.

Home to the famous geyser Old Faithful, Yellowstone Park spreads over three U.S. states—Wyoming, Montana and Idaho.

The park took its name from the fact it's located at the headwaters of the Yellowstone River.

How large is Yellowstone National Park? It's bigger than the entire state of Rhode Island or Delaware.

What was the irony of the name of the high school play that Nancy Reagan was in?

When future first lady Nancy Reagan was in high school in Chicago in 1939 (her name then was Nancy Davis), she was in the senior play at her school, and the name of that play, ironically, happened to be, "The First Lady."

Little did Nancy or her classmates know then that Nancy would later marry Ronald Reagan—and really become the first lady of the land in real life.

A classic puzzler—where is the missing dollar?

Three men get out of their car and check into a motel. The clerk says the room is $30. Each man pays $10, and they go up to the room.

Hours later, the clerk realizes the room rate is only $25, so he sends the bellboy up to the room to refund $5 to the men. The bellboy tries to figure how to split the $5 three ways, so he decides to give each man $1, and the bellboy keeps $2 for himself—so that means each man paid $9 for the room. That's 9 times 3 or $27, and add the $2 the bellboy kept for himself and that gives you a total of $29. WHERE'S THE EXTRA DOLLAR?

It turns out that this is a mathematical anomaly. Mathematicians say there is NO way to account for the extra dollar if you figure it that way—but there is a way to account for it if you figure it another way: Do it this way: The motel got $25. The men each got $1 back so that's $25 plus $3, or $28 and the bellboy kept $2, and that gives you your total of $30. It's all in the way you figure it. If you do it the first way, that total is, oddly, just $29. You would think that mathematically it should come out the same way both times, but it doesn't. And, who said mathematics is an exact science?

What color is ocean water? (Maybe not what you think)

Ask somebody what's the color of ocean water and they'll probably say blue or green. But that's not true.

Contrary to much popular opinion, ocean water really isn't blue or green. It's colorless like other water.

Ocean water only looks blue or green because of reflections from the sky above and from vegetation below.

What's dangerous about the State of the Union address?

Should virtually the entire U.S. government be in the same room at the same time?

When the president gives the State of the Union address to Congress, the vice president is there, the speaker of the House is there, all members of the Congressional leadership and almost all members of Congress are there, most members of the Supreme Court are there, and all members of the cabinet except one are there.

What if something happened, like a fire or terrorist attack? Who would run the government?

One cabinet member is purposely absent, so in case of a catastrophe, that one cabinet member could continue the government, but that seems impractical to put all that on one person—usually a minor cabinet official at that.

Isn't it dangerous to have the entire leadership of the government in the same room at the same time? Something to think about.

What's surprising about the man who wrote the words to the song, "Take Me Out to the Ball Game"?

Jack Norworth, who wrote the words to "Take Me Out to the Ball Game," was not a baseball fan and rarely took himself out to a ball game even though he wrote the most famous baseball song of all.

There are some song historians who say Norworth never even bothered to ever go to a major league baseball game until 1940—and that was 32 years after he wrote the song in 1908.

Ironically, even though Norworth seldom went to games in his lifetime, he's perpetually near a ballpark today. He's buried in a cemetery just across the Interstate from the Los Angeles Angels baseball park in Anaheim, Calif.

What were crossword puzzles supposed to be called?

It's only by mistake that crossword puzzles are called crossword puzzles today.

When Arthur Wynne invented crossword puzzles in 1913 and had his first puzzle published in the New York World newspaper, he called it a wordcross puzzle, but the typesetter made a mistake and accidentally switched "word" and "cross" in the title, making it come out crossword instead of wordcross.

You can almost hear Wynne yelling, "Hey, wait, it's supposed to be wordcross, not crossword." But editors said since it appeared that way in print the first day, it was decided to let it stay that way—thus, one of our most famous names exists by accident.

In case you're wondering, the first clue in Wynne's very first crossword puzzle (1 across) was (5 letters), "What bargain hunters enjoy." The (easy) answer: "sales."

We're used to hearing numbers like millions, billions and sometimes even trillions, but what number comes after trillion?

After million which has six zeros, billion which has nine zeros and trillion which has 12 zeros, comes quadrillion with 15 zeros.

Following quadrillion, it's quintillion with 18 zeros, sextillion with 21 zeros, septillion with 24 zeros, octillion with 27 zeros, nonillion with 30 zeros and decillion with 33 zeros.

What's odd about the names kings and queens go by?

Ever stop to think that kings and queens go by their first names, as in Queen Elizabeth of Great Britain. Why isn't she called Queen Mountbatten, since she is Mrs. Elizabeth Mountbatten, having married Philip Mountbatten—but, kings and queens go by their first name, like King Henry, Queen Victoria, King Louis, etc.

Just think—if presidents did that, we would have been calling recent presidents, President Joe, President Donald, President Barack, President George, President Bill and President Ronald, omitting the last name, like royalty does.

What have been the 5 greatest movie scenes of all time?

It's purely subjective, but these five movie scenes have been picked in a survey as the best and most memorable ever:

The final "goodbye" scene between Humphrey Bogart and Ingrid Bergman in "Casablanca."

The scene in "The Godfather" when a man wakes up and finds in his bed the head of his favorite horse cut off and lying there next to him. (You can still hear him screaming).

Judy Garland singing "Over the Rainbow" in "The Wizard of Oz".

Estelle Reiner, in a restaurant, looking at Meg Ryan's gyrations, telling the waitress, "I'll have what she's having," in "When Harry Met Sally."

Gene Kelly swinging on a lamppost and dancing and singing in the rain in "Singin' in the Rain."

Why is the alert for missing children called an Amber Alert?

Did the Amber Alert get its name from the bright yellow-orange color known as amber? No—the name came from something else.

Amber Alerts are named for a 9-year old girl whose name was Amber Hagerman. She was abducted while riding her bike in Arlington, Texas, in 1996. Her body was later found in a nearby creek.

This tragedy inspired the Amber Alert system now used to alert people to missing children and named in memory of 9-year-old Amber Hagerman.

What are 7 U.S. states that came close to having a different name?

Vermont went by the name New Connecticut for a while, but switched to Vermont before entering the Union.

West Virginia was formed from the northwestern counties of Virginia and could easily have been called North Virginia instead of West Virginia.

As mentioned earlier, Pennsylvania was originally named Sylvania but to pay off a debt owed to William Penn by the king of England, the king added the word Penn to Sylvania, and it became Pennsylvania.

Colorado came close to being named Jefferson in honor of President Thomas Jefferson.

Early settlers in Utah wanted their state to be called Deseret, a word from their Book of Mormon.

The state of Washington almost was called Columbia after the river there.

Hawaii was once called the Sandwich Islands, so the U.S. could have had a state called Sandwich.

Should "she" be added to the U.S. Constitution?

It's surprising in how many places a certain word doesn't appear in the Constitution:

In describing the president's duties, it says he shall have various powers, he shall recommend measures to Congress, and in describing qualifications for members of Congress, it says those elected must be an inhabitant of the state in which he was chosen.

That word "he" appears a lot. As wonderful a job as the Founding Fathers did in writing the Constitution, they failed to consider that sometime the country might have a "she" as president and a "she" or a number of "she's" in Congress.

The question is, should the Constitution be updated to add "she" where now only "he" appears.

How much has U.S. population grown since World War II days?

During World War II, the U.S. was considered a big nation—one of the biggest in the world—and yet, U.S. population then was just 130 million, and that's 200 million less than today.

In other words—and, perhaps surprisingly—U.S. population has more than doubled just since World War II.

An interesting note is that as huge as the U.S. population growth has been over the years, the country still has one of the lowest ratios in the world of people per square mile because of the country's big size. There are just about 89 people per square mile in the U.S. compared to, for example, 267 people per square mile in France, 541 people per square mile in Italy, 649 people per square mile in Pakistan, and places like Bangladesh where they have over 3,000 people per square mile.

On what date did New Year's Day used to be?

Surprisingly, January 1 has not always been the date for New Year's in America.

Before 1752, England and the English colonies—of which America was then one—celebrated New Year's on March 25.

It wasn't changed to January 1 until England and its colonies scrapped the old Julian calendar and adopted the present Gregorian calendar we use today. It was in 1752 that America celebrated New Year's on January 1 for the first time.

And when you stop to think about it, maybe that old March 25 date for New Year's was more logical, after all. March heralds the beginning of spring—and that's really more of a new year than January.

How tall was the tallest animal that ever walked the face of the Earth?

Fossils have been found of dinosaurs known as sauroposeidon who are estimated to have been as tall as a six-story building. How would you like to have seen one of those walking down the road.

Their fossils have been found in parts of what is now Oklahoma, Texas and Wyoming.

What's the best name a football coach could have?

There was once a coach in the National Football League whose name was Charley Winner.

Winner was the head coach of the New York Jets in 1974 and 75—but, sad to say, Winner was not a winner. Despite that great name, Charley Winner was a losing coach, compiling a record of 9 wins and 14 losses with the Jets.

He did better as coach of the Cardinals from 1966 to 1970 where he was a winner with a record of 35 and 30, but alas, Charley Winner's combined career NFL head coaching won-loss total was not a winning record but was overall at 44 and 44.

Still, he had that great name for a coach—Charley Winner.

What major war was started by a 19-year-old student?

It was in June, 1914 that the crown price of the Austria-Hungary empire, Archduke Ferdinand and his wife, made a trip to Sarajevo, Bosnia, then part of the Austria-Hungary empire.

A 19-year-old Serbian student, Gavrilo Princip, who wanted independence for Bosnia, Serbia and other parts of the Balkans, shot and killed the crown prince and his wife.

There was outrage in Austria-Hungary. Austria-Hungary troops then invaded Princip's home country of Serbia—and that set off a chain reaction of events. Other nations that had alliances and treaties with one country or another began choosing sides and joined the fight. Germany and the Ottoman Empire backed Austria-Hungary. Serbia's allies such as Russia, France and Britain backed Serbia and were quickly drawn in. In all, 29 countries, including the United States would eventually battle in what became the biggest war the world had ever seen up to that time—World War I—all started by one 19-year old student.

On that famous HOLLYWOOD sign in the hills above Los Angeles, officials once covered up one of the letters on that sign. What letter was that, and why did they do that?

That HOLLYWOOD sign is 360 feet long and its letters are each 45 feet tall. In September 1987 when Pope John Paul II visited the Los Angeles area, the second "L" was covered up so that the sign read "HOLY WOOD" in the pope's honor.

The sign has been there since 1923 and was originally built by a real estate company to advertise its housing development in the area which they called "Hollywoodland." The sign read "HOLLYWOODLAND" from 1923 until 1949 when part of it blew down. The local chamber of commerce took it over, refurbished it, and had it read just "HOLLYWOOD" from then on—except for covering up that one "L" at the time when the pope visited.

Why do golf courses have 18 holes?

In the early days of golf's development in Scotland, different courses had different numbers of holes.

For example, when the first British Open was played at the Prestwick Club in 1860, that course had only 12 holes. Other courses then had varying numbers of holes—but the most famous course, St. Andrews in Scotland, where royalty played, just happened to have 18 holes because of the space they had for the course.

In the years following, as golf's popularity spread and new courses were built around the world, others made their courses 18 holes just to follow the pattern set by St. Andrews—and 18 holes became the standard for golf courses everywhere.

What was the biggest drunken brawl ever held at the White House?

When Andrew Jackson was inaugurated president in 1829, he invited some tough old buddies and rough frontiersmen he grew up with to come to the White House that evening for a celebration party. What a mistake that was.

Nothing like it has ever been seen at the White House, before or since.

It truly turned into a drunken brawl. Visitors broke glasses, stood on chairs with muddy boots, destroyed furniture, yanked down wall hangings, and fought.

It got so bad, Jackson had to escape through a rear window, and spend his inauguration night at a hotel.

Who was America's first billionaire?

That honor in today's dollars goes to John D. Rockefeller.

Interestingly, Rockefeller was born into a poor family, but he grew up to dominate the oil and railroad industries in the late 1800s and early 1900s, accumulating more wealth than anyone else in America ever had up to that time.

Besides his personal great wealth and eventual philanthropy, Rockefeller left a legacy of political descendants. One grandson, Nelson Rockefeller, was governor of New York and vice president of the United States. Another grandson, Winthrop Rockefeller, was governor of Arkansas. And a great-grandson, Jay Rockefeller, has been a U.S. senator from West Virginia.

What do Germany, Spain, Italy and Norway call themselves—and why don't we call them by those names?

It's interesting how many countries in the world there are that we call by a different name than they call themselves—and it's not a question of difficulty of pronouncing. Here are just a few examples.

For instance, Germany calls itself Deutschland. Why don't we use that name. It's not that hard to pronounce.

Same with Spain. They call their country Espana. We could say that.

Italians call their country Italia. We can say Italia.

Those in Norway call their country Norge. We could certainly say that.

There are other examples—and isn't it strange that we use different names for countries than they use themselves when we really don't have to.

Why is the flu called the flu?

The word flu, of course comes from a shortened version of influenza—but where did that word influenza come from?

Influenza is an Italian word meaning "influence" and in olden days, people thought the disease was caused by the position of the moon and stars, or the "influence" of the moon and stars on humans—and so it was called influenza, after influence.

Incidentally, there was one influenza outbreak in the U.S. that caused a record number of flu deaths. The infamous Spanish flu after World War I, in 1918 and 1919, killed more than 20 million people worldwide and over 500,000 people in the U.S. That flu pandemic killed more people than all those killed in World War I.

Want a sure bet?

Ask a friend to write down any three consecutive numbers from 1 to 9, but not to let you see them. Bet him or her that by special magic you can predict the number they'll get by reversing their three digits and then subtracting the smaller 3-digit number from the larger one.

Amazingly, the answer will ALWAYS be 198, no matter which three consecutive numbers your friend starts with.

For example: Take consecutive numbers 123. Reverse that and you have 321. Subtract 123 from 321 and the answer is 198; Take 567. Reverse that and you have 765. Subtract 567 from 765 and the answer is 198; Take 789. Reverse that and you have 987. Subtract 789 from 987 and the answer is 198. Take 456. Reverse that and you have 654. Subtract 456 from 654 and the answer is 198.

It works every time.

Players on which college football team likely saved their lives by losing a game?

Boston College was the No. 1 college football team in the nation in 1942. They were unbeaten going into their last game against Holy Cross.

They were heavily favored, and made reservations to hold a victory celebration after the game at a nightclub called the Cocoanut Grove in Boston.

However in a big upset, Holy Cross not only beat Boston College, but beat them badly, 55-12. Crushed Boston College officials cancelled the victory party.

That night, the Cocoanut Grove caught fire. It was the deadliest nightclub fire in U.S. history, with 492 people killed.

The Boston College players all might have been killed—except for the fact that they lost a football game that afternoon, and thereby were not at the Cocoanut Grove disaster. They won by losing.

The largest denomination of U.S. paper money is now the $100 bill, but the U.S. once had even larger denominations in general circulation—how big were those bills?

Can you imagine walking around—not with some $10 or $20 bills or even $50 and $100 bills in your purse or wallet or pocket—but with a $5,000 bill or a $10,000 bill?

Did you know the U.S. Treasury once made, and circulated, for a long time, $500, $1,000, $5,000 and $10,000 bills.

In fact, it wasn't until 1969 that they stopped issuing those big denominations.

If you're lucky enough to have any, they're still good but you can't get any more—they're just not made anymore.

Where was the worst hurricane ever to hit the U.S. in terms of fatalities?

The one hurricane that caused the most deaths in U.S. history was the one that hit the Galveston, Texas, area on Sept. 8, 1900.

The toll from that hurricane was an estimated 6,000 to 9,000 people killed.

How did such a relatively small country as Britain once get such a big empire, and then what happened?

It's truly amazing how big the British Empire once was. It's all the more amazing when you consider that Britain's home island is smaller than the U.S. state of Oregon—yet the British were able to control so much of the world.

Here are just some of the countries today that were once British colonies, and part of the British Empire:

There's India, Australia, New Zealand, Singapore, Malaysia, Hong Kong, Egypt, South Africa, Sudan, Somalia, Kenya, Nigeria, Ireland and Canada, to name just a few. And let's not forget the United States.

The British had possessions in virtually every time zone throughout the world, leading to the statement that the sun never set on the British Empire.

So, how did that one, little country get control of, and rule, so many other places?

It was a combination of several things, beginning in the 1600s.

The British, being on an island, developed expert seamanship and the desire to explore. From that they developed not only the desire to explore, but also to settle (and conquer if necessary) as many lands as possible for commercial gain and to bring imports from around the world to their homeland—things they didn't have or were unable to grow at home.

They also found great new wealth in their newly-found commercial trading around the world. At the same time, they were developing a feeling of superiority—a feeling that their way of life was best for other countries.

Then, what happened to the British Empire?

The empire began to break up in the 20th century. Devastating losses of so many of its young men in World War I, more all-out fighting in World War II to save its homeland, then changing times with cries for independence from many former colonies, plus perhaps a tiredness of it all, led the British, in most cases, peacefully and without fighting, to voluntarily give up many of its lands, including the nation with the second-largest population in the world, India.

Now, the once-great British Empire is reduced to just a fraction of its former self.

What were all the basic things invented in one magical 27-year period, 1876 to 1903?

In those 27 years, all these things were created—automobiles, movies, radio, airplanes, the phonograph and the telephone.

Before 1876 none of those things existed. After 1903, they all did.

What a creative period that was.

Which U.S. president once played in the world series?

Well, it was the college baseball world series—but that's still pretty good.

President George H. W. Bush was not only the starting first baseman for the Yale University team, but was also the captain of the team—and Bush's Yale team played in the first two college baseball world series, in 1947 and 1948.

Yale reached the finals both years, losing to California in 1947 and Southern California in 1948.

There are 10 countries in the world that have just 4 letters in their name. What are those countries?

Of the 10 countries in the world that have just 4-letter names, two are in the Americas—Cuba and Peru.

In the Middle East, there's Iran, Iraq and Oman.

In Africa there's Chad, Mali and Togo.

In Southeast Asia, there's Laos, and in the Pacific, there's the island nation of Fiji.

What animals can outlive humans?

Amazingly, there are some kinds of animals that, despite the fact they don't have medical knowledge or medicines, can outlive humans by many years.

Humans, with all our medical knowledge and modern medicines cannot, for instance, outlive many kinds of turtles. Some turtles live to age 150 and beyond.

There are clams, oysters, jellyfish and whales that are believed to live as long as 200 years and more.

How is it that without the benefit of modern medical science, these animals can have such a long life span?

What were potato chips originally called?

They weren't called potato chips for many years.

Potato chips were created at a resort hotel in Saratoga Springs, N.Y., in 1853 by a chef there whose name, incidentally and appropriately, was George Crum.

Chef Crum created potato chips and they became a specialty of the Saratoga Springs Hotel…and were called Saratoga chips.

Their popularity gradually spread around the country with the name Saratoga chips. They were called Saratoga chips, and not potato chips, for many years, even into the 1900s.

It took a long time for those chips to lose their place of origin and be called potato chips instead of Saratoga chips.

What was the profession of the man who wrote "The Star-Spangled Banner?"

Francis Scott Key, who wrote the words to "The Star-Spangled Banner," was not a song writer.

He was a lawyer, and later in his life a district attorney in the Washington, D.C. area.

It was as a lawyer that Key was on the scene in Baltimore during the War of 1812 to see the Battle for Ft. McHenry. He was there to negotiate the release of a prisoner held by the British.

Key watched the bombardment of the fort by the British all night, and then at dawn on Sept. 14, 1814, Key saw that the American flag was still flying over the fort. That inspired him to take an envelope out of his pocket and begin to write the immortal words that started with, "Oh say can you see by the dawn's early light...".

What are the incredible number of tragedies that struck the Kennedy family?

The family of Rose and Joseph Kennedy was blessed with wealth, privilege, and power—yet that family was the victim of an unbelievable number of tragedies:

The eldest son, Joseph Jr., died in a plane crash in World War II.

The eldest daughter, Rosemary, was mentally ill and institutionalized for life following a failed lobotomy.

Another daughter, Kathleen, died in a plane crash.

Sons John and Robert Kennedy were both assassinated, John while U.S. president, and Robert while a U.S. senator.

Another son, Ted, drove off a bridge, and Mary Jo Kopechine, an aide who was with him, died in the accident.

Edward Kennedy Jr., Ted's son, lost his right leg to cancer.

Joseph Kennedy, son of Robert, was the driver of a car that was in an accident and left one passenger permanently paralyzed.

David Kennedy, also a son of Robert, died of a drug overdose.

Michael Kennedy, another son of Robert, was killed when he crashed into a tree while skiing.

John Kennedy Jr., son of President Kennedy, was killed in a plane crash along with his wife and sister-in-law.

Meantime, Rose Kennedy, the mother of Joe Jr., Rosemary, Kathleen, John, Robert and Ted, lived through much of this until her death in 1995. Despite enduring so many of these tragedies, Rose lived a long life—to age 104—just the opposite of many of her children and grandchildren.

What are 3 words understood in virtually all languages?

Wherever you go in the world, whatever language is spoken there, there are three words we use all the time that are understood just about everywhere.

One word is "OK," a word that originated in America in the 1800s and is now used all over the world.

Another is "amen," used in many different religions.

And the third word is "taxi,"—a word used in most countries.

So, you'll probably be understood if you say "OK," "amen," or "taxi" just about anywhere you go.

What was the infamous "3 Eddies" play in baseball?

It was one of the zaniest plays in a big league baseball game.

In a game in 1948, Eddie Stevens was playing first base for the Pittsburgh Pirates, Eddie Bockman was playing third and Eddie Fitzgerald was catching.

The batter hit a pop fly near the mound. Eddie Stevens came over from first, Eddie Bockman from third, and Eddie Fitzgerald from behind the plate toward the ball.

The pitcher, forgetting that all three players had the same first name, shouted, "Eddie, you take it."

All three Eddies, looking up at the ball, crashed into each other. The ball fell to the ground for a base hit.

What famous people have the name of a food in their name?

There was former Secretary of State Condoleezza Rice, actors Kevin Bacon, Jack Lemon and John Candy, actress Halle Berry, U.S. Supreme Court justices Felix Frankfurter and Warren Burger, U.S. Congressman Anthony Weiner, clothing manufacturer L.L. Bean, baseball players Mike Trout, Daryl Strawberry and Coco Crisp, women's soccer star Mia Hamm, and of course, singer Meatloaf.

You can have some enjoyment trying to think of some more.

Which 4 months have the wrong name?

The four of our months that really have a wrong name are September, October, November and December.

According to their Latin derivation, September means seventh month, October means eighth, November means ninth and December means tenth month—but September is our ninth month, October is tenth, November eleventh and December is our twelfth month.

The confusion came when the calendar was changed many years ago.

Positions of the months were changed with September moving from being the seventh month to now being the ninth month, October moved from being the eighth month to now being the tenth month, November moved from being the ninth month to now being the eleventh month, and December moved from being the tenth month to now being the twelfth month, but nobody bothered to change their names, and their really wrong names exist today.

The first parking meters in the U.S. were installed in Oklahoma City—and what was the coincidence about the street where they were first installed?

Parking meters were invented and patented by Carl Magee, a member of the Oklahoma City traffic committee, in 1935.

By coincidence, the name of the street in Oklahoma City where the first parking meters were placed was…Park Avenue.

After those first parking meters were installed on Park Avenue, many motorists came there and parked by the meters on purpose (and paid their nickels)—just to see how the meters worked.

When did the U.S. have the possibility of 2 presidents named JFK?

John Fitzgerald Kennedy, the U.S. president from 1961 to 1963, was familiarly known by his initials, JFK—but another JFK later ran for president.

In the 2004 presidential election, the Democratic nominee was John Kerry whose middle name is Forbes, so his initials are also JFK. When Kerry attended Yale University during the time that Kennedy was U.S. president, Kerry was often compared to Kennedy.

They were both from prominent New England families, both interested in politics, and both with the initials of JFK. The only thing is, Kerry lost his presidential election (to George W. Bush) and the country did not have two JFK presidents.

What are the 10 U.S. states that have 2-word names?

It turns out that 20 percent of all U.S. states—10 of the 50—have two-word names, and here they are, alphabetically:

New Hampshire
New Jersey
New Mexico
New York
North Carolina
North Dakota
Rhode Island
South Carolina
South Dakota
West Virginia.

What was the first college in America west of the Mississippi?

It's generally well-known that Harvard, in Cambridge, Mass., was the first college established in America, and all the other early colleges in America were also all east of the Mississippi River, but a much tougher question is—what was the first college ever established west of the Mississippi? Of all the colleges and universities west of the Mississippi today, which one was first?

The first college west of the Mississippi was… St. Louis University in St. Louis, Mo.. It was established in 1818 by the Jesuits.

St. Louis University exists today with over 13,000 students, and of all the colleges west of the Mississippi, it was the first.

Has anyone in the past ever had your Social Security number?

A common question the Social Security Administration gets is: With all the millions of people in the country having Social Security numbers now, and with all those deceased people having had Social Security numbers in the past, is it possible—with just the nine numbers that Social Security numbers have—that anyone else has ever had your number?

It turns out there are enough possible combinations in the nine-digit system to allow for about one-billion unique Social Security numbers. About 500-million numbers have been issued since the program began, so they won't run out of combinations for quite a while, and no one else apparently has had the same number that you have.

When they eventually do run out of unique combinations, the government might reissue numbers of those who died long ago, or go to a 10- or-11-digit system. But as of now, your Social Security number is yours, and yours alone.

Which team made the World Series 22 times in one 29-year period?

It's an amazing, almost unbelievable record.

There was one period of 29 consecutive years when one team made the World Series in 22 of those years.

From 1936 through 1964—29 straight years—the New York Yankees were in the World Series 22 times. The Yankees made the World Series in 1936, 1937, 1938, 1939, 1941, 1942, 1943, 1947, 1949, 1950, 1951, 1952, 1953, 1955, 1956, 1957, 1958, 1960, 1961, 1962,1963 and 1964.

No other major league baseball team has ever come close to that record.

Who were the 10 U.S. presidents with the same last name as another U.S. president?

It's a bit hard to believe when you first hear it, but there have been 10 U.S. presidents with the same last name as another U.S. president.

There's John Adams and John Quincy Adams, William Henry Harrison and Benjamin Harrison, Andrew Johnson and Lyndon Johnson, Theodore Roosevelt and Franklin Roosevelt, and George H.W. Bush and George W. Bush.

That's over 20 percent of all U.S. presidents with the same last name as another U.S. president.

Are most fire trucks, fire plugs, police cars and other emergency vehicles the right color?

Maybe not.

Studies have shown that the most visible color is not red, as fire trucks and fire plugs in many cities and towns are, and it's not white as police cars and emergency vehicles often are in many places.

Those studies show that the most visible color is yellow, and while some places have adopted that color, many others have not. Red for fire trucks, for instance, is an old tradition that started before modern studies on color.

It might be a good idea to consider switching to yellow.

Can you imagine the federal government ordering U.S. automakers to stop making new cars?   When did that happen?

What would people say today if, all of a sudden, the federal government told U.S. automakers, "You can't make any more new cars, and people will have to do without." Well, that once really happened.

It was during World War II when the government ordered all U.S. automakers to stop making cars for the general public and, instead, convert their factories to producing war materials.

The ban preventing U.S. automakers from making new cars lasted three years, from 1942 to 1945, and by and large, the American public readily accepted the ban for the good of the war effort.

What word becomes shorter when you ADD 2 letters to it?

That word is short.

Add two letters…and it's shorter

Which country in the world has the tallest people?

The country with the tallest people is the Netherlands where the average height of adult males is just over 6 feet and the average height of adult females is 5-7.

After the Netherlands come Denmark, Finland, Germany and Sweden.

Some African nations have especially tall people but that is countered with a good number of shorter people also in those countries which brings down the average height for the countries as a whole, so the Netherlands is No. 1 in average height.

Who was the first U.S. president to face an assassination attempt by a woman?

Gerald Ford was not only the first U.S. president ever to face an assassination attempt by a woman, but he faced yet another such attack from yet another woman in just one incredible 17-day period.

On Sept. 5, 1975, Ford was coming out of a hotel in Sacramento, Calif., after giving a speech, when Lynette "Squeaky" Fromme aimed a pistol at Ford. A secret service agent grabbed the pistol before Fromme could fire it.

Then 17 days later, Ford was coming out of a hotel in San Francisco after giving a speech there when Sara Jane Moore fired a pistol at Ford. A bystander pushed her arm and caused the bullet to miss Ford.

Miraculously, Ford escaped unharmed in both assassination attempts in that September of 1975.

Why did those women want to shoot a president?

Lynette "Squeaky" Fromme was a follower of cult leader Charles Manson. Manson had convinced her that he was the Messiah and the goal was to kill celebrities. After Manson was sent to prison for murdering actress Sharon Tate, Fromme wanted to carry on Manson's work and commit a famous crime. (Squeaky's nickname was given to her because of her high-pitched voice).

Sara Jane Moore was a former employee of the FBI. She had been active in the counterculture movement in California and had been recruited by the FBI to gain inside information on the kidnapping of newspaper heiress Patty Hearst by a counterculture group. After Moore's friends found out she was working for the FBI, they turned against her. Wanting to reconnect with her friends, Moore decided to try to shoot the president to show her friends she was still with them.

After Ford escaped those two assassination attempts, he came up with a classic line, "Luckily I'm a Ford, not a Lincoln."

For what movie did its star have to go on a real-life eating binge to gain 60 pounds while the movie was being shot?

During the making of the movie "Raging Bull" about boxer Jake LaMotta, actor Robert De Niro had to gain 60 pounds to accurately portray LaMotta's transition from a middleweight boxing champion to a bloated older man.

After shooting the first part of the movie with De Niro at his normal weight, they shut down filming for four months so De Niro could go on an eating binge and gain 60 pounds to show the older LaMotta.

De Niro went from 150 pounds to 210. That is said to be the most weight any actor ever had to gain for a film. The movie was highly honored. The American Film Institute voted it the fourth greatest American movie of all time, and De Niro won the Oscar for Best Actor for his portrayal of LaMotta.

What are the only 2 letters of the alphabet not used in the spelling of any of our numbers?

At first thought, a person might think of least-used letters like "q," "x" and "z"—but those letters are used in the spelling of numbers. "Q" is used in the spelling of some big numbers like quadrillion and quintillion, "x" is used in six, and "z" is used in zero. The only two letters not used in the spelling of ANY of our numbers are "j" and "k".

Can you imagine the leader of a country having the name "Goodluck" as his real name?

Leaders of countries need good luck, and if ever a person has had a great name for that job, it's the man who became president of Nigeria in 2010.

His name: Goodluck Jonathan. That is his real name.

Goodluck Jonathan was born in Nigeria in 1957 and served in various political jobs there, including being an education minister, governor of a Nigerian state, and vice president, before becoming president,

And, his wife has maybe the best name for any woman who has been first lady of a country. Her first name is Patience.

Could it be that the coldest outdoor temperature ever recorded on Earth happened in July or August?

There's an oddity about the coldest outdoor temperature ever recorded anywhere in the world.

That record was set, of all months, in July. The reason, of course, is that July is a winter month in the Southern Hemisphere, and the record was set in Antarctica which is in the Southern Hemisphere.

The official all-time low was 129 below zero Fahrenheit at Vostok, Antarctica, on July 21, 1983. There's also an unconfirmed record of 136 below in August in Antarctica.

Coldest it's ever been in the U.S. since weather bureau records began to be kept, was 80 below at Prospect Creek, Alaska, Jan. 23, 1971. The record cold in the lower 48 states is 70 below at Rogers Pass, Mont., on Jan. 20, 1954.

What sports stars have been elected to high government offices?

A member of the baseball Hall of Fame was elected to the U.S. Senate—that was former big league pitcher Jim Bunning who was a U.S. senator from Kentucky.

There was also a member of the basketball Hall of Fame elected to the U.S. Senate—NBA star Bill Bradley, a U.S. senator from New Jersey.

College and pro football stars who have served in the U.S. House of Representatives include Steve Largent of Oklahoma, Jack Kemp of New York, J.C. Watts of Oklahoma, Heath Shuler of North Carolina, plus famed coach Tom Osborne from Nebraska. Also elected to the House were track star Jim Ryan of Kansas and Olympic decathlon champion Bob Mathias of California. Hockey Hall of Fame goalie Ken Dryden was elected to the Canadian parliament.

Body-building champion Arnold Schwarzenegger was governor of California and wrestling champ Jesse Ventura was governor of Minnesota.

And let's not forget a football star reached the White House. He played on two national championship teams at the University of Michigan and was offered tryouts by two NFL teams—President Gerald Ford.

What's the largest minority in the United States?

The largest minority in the U.S. are...males.

The majority of people in the U.S. are female. 50.8 percent of the population is female. That biggest minority are males, with 49.2 percent of the population being male.

The interesting thing is that more boys are born each year than girls. Women of all races give birth to about 106 boys for every 100 girls. But in the total population, there are more females than males because women, on average, live longer than men—so females are the majority in the country, and males are the biggest minority.

Of all the people who have ever run for political offices in the U.S., which one got the most total votes in a lifetime?

The answer may be a surprise.

The person who's gotten the most total votes on election days in U.S. history is...Richard Nixon.

One reason is that he ran for so many different national offices— running for the U.S. House of Representatives twice, the U.S. Senate once, vice president twice, president three times, plus one race for governor of California.

He got over 170 million votes all together on election days, and no one else has ever gotten more.

How did Santa Claus get that name?

Santa is known by lots of different names around the world—
names like Father Christmas and Papa Noel, but here's how he
became known as Santa Claus in America.

When Dutch settlers came to America in the 1600s, they brought
their name, Sinter Klaus, or the good saint, and that name Sinter
Klaus then evolved in America into Santa Claus.

The original Santa was the real St. Nicholas in the 4th century who
lived in what is now Turkey. He was from a wealthy family and
became famous for giving gifts—and in coming years as the stories
of his gift-giving spread, the name of that real St. Nicholas
changed into many different names around the world, including
Sinter Klaus, and now our Santa Claus.

What major city has changed its name 3 times since 1914?

One of the world's best-known cities is St. Petersburg, Russia—
but, wait, is that really its name? It's had its name changed so
much, you really can't be sure.

St. Petersburg was originally named St. Petersburg after its
founder, Czar Peter the Great. But then in World War I, the
Russians wanted a more Russian-sounding name for St.
Petersburg, so they changed its name to Petrograd.

In 1924 with the Soviets controlling Russia, they then wanted to
honor their leader, Lenin, so it was goodbye Petrograd and hello

Leningrad as the city's name changed from Petrograd to Leningrad.

It remained Leningrad until the Soviet Union collapsed in 1991 and the city's name was changed yet again, this time back to the original St. Petersburg.

That's a lot of changes for one city's name.

Why is Theodore Roosevelt with Washington, Jefferson and Lincoln on Mt. Rushmore?

A famous site in America are the spectacular sculptures on Mt. Rushmore, in South Dakota, showing faces of four U.S. presidents—but there's a lingering question about one of those presidents.

The presidents depicted on Mt. Rushmore are George Washington, Thomas Jefferson, Abraham Lincoln and Theodore Roosevelt— and there's no question why Washington, Jefferson and Lincoln are there. They're considered three of the greatest presidents, but tour guides are often asked: Why is Theodore Roosevelt there? Tour guides say they get that question more than any other.

Theodore Roosevelt was a popular president, but is he in the same class as Washington, Jefferson and Lincoln?

It turns out that the sculptor of the faces on Mt. Rushmore, Gutzon Borglum, took the job with the provision that he could pick which four presidents would be shown. Roosevelt happened to be a personal favorite of his, and that's why Theodore Roosevelt is included with Washington, Jefferson and Lincoln.

Where did the word "news" come from?

There are a couple of theories on why the news is called the news.

One theory is that the word "news" came from taking the first letters of north, east, west and south—n-e-w-s, since news comes from all over. That's a creative thought, but most word historians dismiss that as the origin.

The most generally accepted theory is that the word "news" simply came from the plural of the word "new."

How did the city of Newport News, Va., get that name—and is the newspaper there simply called The Newport News?

There's a nice story on how that Virginia city got its unique name.

Soon after the area was originally settled in the 1600s by British colonists, they encountered a food shortage and were ready to leave. Just then, a ship captained by Christopher Newport brought them supplies, and that was called "Newport's good news," leading the colonists to begin to call the area "Newport's News. Eventually, the "s" after Newport's name was dropped and the settlement became Newport News.

All of which leads to the question of what the daily newspaper there is called. It could be called simply, The Newport News. But, alas, it doesn't use that name. It's the Newport News Daily Press.

What are the largest birds in the world today?

The answer to this may be a surprise.

The largest birds today are the ostriches.

Some ostriches reach eight feet in height and weigh as much as 350 pounds. That's big for a bird.

How many years did the NFL exist without having the Super Bowl?

The NFL was in existence for a long time before the first Super Bowl game was ever played.

It seems hard to believe now, but the NFL was around for 47 years before they staged the first Super Bowl.

The NFL started in 1920—but the first Super Bowl wasn't played until 1967.

In all those years when there was no Super Bowl, the NFL called their end-of-the-season championship game simply, the NFL championship game. Not very catchy, but that's the way it was.

Tickets at that first Super Bowl, by the way, could be had for just $12, and there were 30,000 empty seats at Super Bowl I. Times have changed.

Why are buffalo wings called buffalo wings even though they're made of chicken and not buffalo meat?

Buffalo wings were created one night in 1984 by Teresa Bellassimo at the Anchor Bar in Buffalo, N.Y.

Some customers came in late and wanted something to eat. Teresa didn't have much food left, but did have some chicken wings which she quickly cooked up and served. The customers liked them, and that became a specialty of Teresa's Anchor Bar which she owned with her husband, Frank.

Since that chicken wing specialty was created in Buffalo, N.Y., they called them buffalo wings even though they're made of chicken, and not buffalo meat.

What are some words that if you spell them exactly backward, you get a completely new word?

One example is the word desserts. Spell it backward, and you get stressed.

Another example is the word was. Spell it backward and you have saw.

Take the word parts. Spell it backward and you have strap.

How about diaper. Spell that backward and you have repaid.

Then there's drawer. Spell that backward and you have reward.

Thinking of combinations like this can make for a good game, and a good mental exercise.

What incredible event happened in Tokyo, Japan, on Sept. 1, 1923, and led to an amazing recovery?

The biggest earthquake ever to hit a major city in modern times struck Tokyo on that September day in 1923, and, incredibly, killed over 100,000 people and left more than two million people homeless. The earthquake caused thousands of buildings and homes to collapse, crushing people, and then there was a firestorm that swept across the city that caused more deaths and damage. BUT, that's not the end of the story.

Amazingly, Tokyo quickly rebuilt after that, and then, in World War II, in the 1940s, U.S. bombers bombed Tokyo, and again many of its buildings and homes were destroyed. Again, rubble everywhere. Today you'd never know it.

Tokyo again recovered and rebuilt, and now it's not only the biggest city in the world, but one of the most bustling and thriving, with thousands of new buildings, lots of neon lights everywhere, and millions of people moving about. Tokyo's metro-area population today is over 30 million.

Two incredible comebacks by Tokyo.

How really big is Alaska?

There's an amazing fact about how big in size the U.S. state of Alaska is.

Of the 196 independent countries of the world, Alaska is bigger than 178 of them.

Alaska is bigger than all but 18 countries in the world.

For example, Alaska is bigger than France or Germany or Spain or Italy or Iraq or Turkey or Pakistan or Egypt or Japan.

Did a U.S. presidential election ever end in a tie?

Surprisingly, an election for president of the United States once did end in a tie.

It happened when Thomas Jefferson and Aaron Burr each received exactly the same number of Electoral College votes in the 1800 election—and, of course, it's Electoral College votes that decide a presidential election.

Under the Constitution, because it was a tie, it was referred to the House of Representatives to choose the winner, and the House then chose Jefferson president.

It could happen again because, for one thing, in the Electoral College there's an even number of electoral votes today, 538, and with that even number you could have a tie if each candidate got 269 electoral votes. Perhaps it might help if the total number of electoral votes was changed from an even number—538—to an odd number. There could still be a tie with an odd number if, say, one elector did not vote or voted for a third-party candidate, but the chances of a tie would be reduced with an odd number of electoral votes.

When did the way we board airplanes change drastically?

It seems hard to believe now, but there was a time, for many years, when if you wanted to fly somewhere on a commercial airline, you could just walk through the gate, walk to your plane and get on. No security people. No metal detectors, No security lines. No inspection of you or your baggage.

That was true from the beginning of commercial air service in the early 1900s until the early 1970s.

It all began to change when a man identified as D.B. Cooper boarded a plane in Portland, Ore., in 1971. Once airborne, he gave a note to a flight attendant saying he had a bomb in his briefcase and would blow up the plane if he didn't receive $200,000 when the plane landed in Seattle. Cooper got his money upon landing, released the other passengers, and instructed the flight crew to take off again with just him and the crew aboard. After a short flight over Washington state, he jumped out of the plane with a parachute he had also demanded, and with the $200,000 in cash.

Cooper was never found or seen again, dead or alive, and his disappearance has remained one of the great enduring mysteries—but he did leave his mark on all future commercial air travel, creating the beginning of tight security when people board airplanes.

Why are the U.S. colors red, white and blue?

During the early years of the Revolutionary War, the U.S. had no official flag and no official colors. Troops carried flags of different designs and different colors.

Then on June 14, 1777, the Continental Congress passed a resolution authorizing a flag of red, white and blue with stars and stripes as the official flag of the United States.

A Congressional resolution said those colors were chosen to designate red for hardiness and courage, white for purity, and blue for vigilance and justice.

What are the only 2 U.S. state capital cities whose names end in "u"?

There's an oddity to the answer of this question.

The only two U.S. state capital cities whose names end in the letter "u" are the capitals of the last two states to join the Union.

Those capital cities are Juneau, Alaska, and Honolulu, Hawaii.

No other U.S. state capitals end in "u."

Why is the AK-47 assault rifle called AK-47?

The AK-47 assault rifle is the most widely used in the world with over 100 million worldwide.

Its name came about this way:

The rifle was developed by Mikhail Kalashnikov of Russia. After several years of testing, Kalashnikov perfected the rifle in 1947, so the name of the rifle became AK-47, with the "A" coming from the first letter of the word "assault," the "K" coming from the first letter of Kalashnikov's last name, and the "47" coming from the last two numbers of the year Kalashnikov perfected the rifle, 1947, hence AK-47.

After creating the rifle, Kalashnikov became a general in the Russian army. He died in 2013 at age 94.

What was odd about the name people called their close associates and friends in the 1800s?

That odd custom was to call close associates and friends only by their last name—and never their first name. One example of that strange custom involved the man who invented the telephone, Alexander Graham Bell. While working on creating the telephone, Bell had an associate named Thomas Watson. They worked closely together. One day in 1876, Thomas Watson was in one room and Alexander Graham Bell was in the adjoining room, testing the phones. So far, the phones hadn't worked. But then that day, as Watson was in one room and Bell in the adjoining one, Bell spilled some acid on his leg. It was painful, and Bell shouted into the phone, "Mr. Watson, come here, I need you." Watson, in the next room, heard Bell and quickly came into assist him.

That was a historic moment because it turned out to be the first telephone call in history—Watson heard Bell through the telephone, proving that the phone worked and their latest experiment was successful, BUT, you would have thought that Bell would have said, "Tom, come here, I need you." No—he called him "Mr. Watson" even though they had been working closely together for months.

In another example of that, in the fictional Sherlock Holmes stories, even though Sherlock Holmes and his associate Dr. John Watson worked closely together and actually lived together at times, Sherlock Holmes never called John Watson, John. It was always, "Watson." And Watson always called Holmes, "Holmes," never Sherlock. You'd think two people that close would call each other by their first names, but that example from the Sherlock Holmes stories was the way it was in those times. Even though Sherlock Holmes was fictional, it was typical of real life then.

Also in that quaint custom of using only last names, there was the famous real-life encounter of newspaper man Henry Stanley and explorer Dr. David Livingstone in 1871. Livingstone, who was trying to find the source of the Nile River, had not been heard from in months, and Henry Stanley was sent by his newspaper on an assignment to try to find Livingstone. Henry Stanley had been searching all through the wilds of Africa in a well-publicized day-after-day adventure to locate David Livingstone. Finally, Henry Stanley spotted him. Henry Stanley assumed it was Livingstone because this man he saw was the only white man he had seen in his long search for Livingstone through central Africa. As soon as Henry Stanley saw the man he assumed was David Livingstone, Henry Stanley didn't say, "David, is that you?" or "Hi David, I've been looking all over for you." No, he made the immortal greeting, "Dr. Livingstone, I presume."

One last note on that: Even movie actor Spencer Tracy, who played Henry Stanley in the movie about Stanley and Livingstone, said he was embarrassed to say that line because it was so corny and pompous. But that's the way they talked in those times.

What's the oddity about the dates on which Presidents Kennedy, Johnson and Nixon died?

You may remember the amazing oddity we wrote about earlier in this book—the oddity that three of the first five U.S. presidents, John Adams, Thomas Jefferson and James Monroe, all died, by coincidence, on the same date, July 4, all of unrelated causes. (Adams and Jefferson both died on July 4, 1826, and Monroe died on July 4, 1831). Well, we just found another one of those coincidences.

Three consecutive presidents—the 35th, 36th and 37th presidents, John Kennedy, Lyndon Johnson and Richard Nixon—all, by coincidence, died on the same date of the month, again all of unrelated causes.

Kennedy died on the 22nd of November, 1963, Johnson died on the 22nd of January, 1973, and Nixon died on the 22nd of April, 1994.

What are the odds on that?

Which U.S. state has a misleading name?

Rhode Island is not an island. The vast majority of the state is on the mainland.

Exactly how it got its misleading name is not known. One theory is that Italian explorer Giovanni de Verrazano thought it resembled the Greek island of Rhodes and gave it that name. Another theory is that Dutch explorer Adrien Block saw its red clay and named it with the Dutch phrase for red clay, "Roode Eylandt," and that name evolved into Rhode Island.

There's a town in America called Boring--how did it get that name?

Boring is a town of about 8,000 population in Oregon, about 20 miles southeast of Portland.

Why was that town given the name of Boring?

It was named after an early settler whose name happened to be, William H. Boring.

Today, with tongue in cheek, the motto of the town is, "Boring, a Most Exciting Place To Live."

There's also a town in Scotland named Dull. It got that name from an old Gaelic word meaning meadow.

What's the U.S. record for the most snow in one place in one day?

In the history of weather bureau records, the record for the greatest one-day snowfall in the United States was set at Silver Lake, Colo., on April 14, 1921.

How much did it snow then?

In 24 hours, more than 6 feet of snow came down. The official total was 76 inches in 24 hours for the all-time high.

Who are some famous people who are not royalty--yet have first or last royal names, like King, Queen, Prince, etc.?

Here are a few to get you started:

Author Stephen King, singer-actress Queen Latifah, Broadway producer Harold Prince, Musician Duke Ellington, football Hall of Famer Earl Campbell, former major league baseball player Marquis Grissom, musician Count Basie and comic book villain Baron Zemo.

How many years did the U.S. go with the cost of a first-class postage stamp not being higher than 3 cents?

Would you believe the U.S. once went 95 consecutive years with a first-class stamp costing no more than 3 cents.

It was 3 cents in 1863 and still 3 cents in 1957.

The rate finally went up to 4 cents in 1958—and people complained about that then.

Once the 4-cent first-class stamp went into effect in 1958, the price kept going up regularly every few years after that, although it didn't reach 10 cents until 1974, 20 cents in 1981, 30 cents in the 1990s and a price in the 40s in 2007, going up regularly in small increments every few years.

How did lollipops get that name?

The candy on a stick that we call a lollipop was developed by a man named George Smith in the early 1900s—and he came up with that distinctive name of lollipop in an unusual way.

Smith named his candy on a stick after a famous and popular racehorse at that time whose name was Lolly Pop.

What player changed the way NFL helmets look?

Fred Gehrke, a running back for the Los Angeles Rams in the National Football League   in 1948, had majored in art in college, and got the idea of painting a picture of a ram's horn on his team's helmets. Up to then, helmets in the NFL had no designs.

After Gehrke hand-painted a ram's horn on all his team's helmets, the Rams became the first NFL team to have a distinctive logo on their helmets. Fans liked it and other NFL teams followed with designs of their own on their helmets.

Gehrke didn't make a lot of money for creating a new look in the NFL. He was paid $1 each for painting the Rams helmets—so for his revolutionary idea, he made about $50, but he also made history.

Are these really wrong answers?

A listener to our radio program once sent us some test questions that students supposedly got a zero on, but maybe they should have gotten 100 percent for their witty answers:

Q: In which battle did General George Custer die? A: His last battle

Q: Are there any U.S. presidents who are not buried in the United States? A: Yes, the current president and all living ex-presidents.

Q: The Miami River flows in which state? A: Liquid

Q: Where was the Declaration of Independence signed? A: At the bottom of the page.

Of all the weddings ever held in America, which one drew the biggest crowd?

When President Theodore Roosevelt's daughter Alice married U.S. Congressman Nicholas Longworth at the White House in 1906, there was a huge crowd of invitees inside the White House—and thousands more people who gathered outside around the White House to be part of the scene and to try to view the bride and groom when they left for their honeymoon. It is said there were more people at that wedding than any other in U.S. history.

Alice chose a blue gown as her wedding dress, and that shade of blue was quickly called Alice blue. Later, a popular song was written that became a standard—"In Her Sweet Little Alice Blue Gown."

Which 3 federal holidays used to have different names?

Memorial Day was originally called Decoration Day—for a very good reason. The holiday started in Civil War times when people took this day to "decorate" graves of servicemen killed in the war, so for many years it was called Decoration Day. As time went on, groups like the American Legion campaigned to "memorialize" servicemen and women who died in all wars, and the name of the holiday gradually began to be called Memorial Day. Congress made the name change official in 1971 and moved the holiday from its original May 30 to the last Monday of May each year.

Veterans Day began as Armistice Day after World War I, celebrating the day of that war's armistice, Nov. 11, 1918. After World War II, veterans groups campaigned to have the name of the holiday changed to Veterans Day to honor all veterans, and the change was made in 1954.

The third federal holiday to have its name changed is Washington's Birthday. It was moved by Congress in 1971 from its original February 22 date to the third Monday of February each year to give us another three-day holiday weekend, and the day is now usually called Presidents Day instead of Washington's Birthday.

The biggest city in population in one U.S. state has exactly the same name as the biggest city in population in another U.S. state. What is that name, and what are the states?

The biggest city in Oregon is Portland—and the biggest city in Maine is also named Portland.

Some readers might have guessed Kansas City, which is in both Kansas and Missouri. But although Kansas City is the biggest city in Missouri, it's not the biggest city in Kansas. Wichita is.

What is the most-eaten vegetable in the U.S., and what's the most-eaten fruit?

The most eaten vegetable in the U.S. is the potato.

Many people might guess apples or oranges for the most-eaten fruit, but the answer is the banana.

A major league baseball player once caught his own home run in a game—how's that possible?

It happened to Dixie Walker of the Dodgers one day in their old ballpark, Ebbets Field in Brooklyn, in 1947.

Walker hit a home run, with the ball sticking in, and staying in, the screen high above the right field fence.

At the end of the inning, Walker went out to play his position in right field, and as he neared the fence, the ball suddenly started to drop out of the screen. Walker ran over, caught the ball, and became the only player in history who caught his own home run.

How did Franklin Roosevelt, the longest-serving U.S. president, come within inches of never serving at all?

Seventeen days before Roosevelt was to be inaugurated for his first term in 1933, he was in Miami to give a speech. Roosevelt was at the podium, standing alongside other officials, and ready to give his speech when an unemployed brick layer, Giuseppe Zangara, tried to assassinate Roosevelt. (Zangara said at his trial that he had wanted to kill kings and presidents).

Zangara fired a shot at Roosevelt, but his shot just missed Roosevelt, by inches, and instead, hit, and killed, the man standing right next to Roosevelt, the mayor of Chicago, Anton Cermak. Zangara then quickly fired more shots and again missed Roosevelt but wounded five other people.

Roosevelt was unharmed, but came that incredibly close to never being president at all. What a difference a few inches made.

Why is there a pyramid on the back of U.S. $1 bills when the U.S. is not known for pyramids?

The Great Seal of the United States is on the back of $1 bills—and on the Seal is a pyramid. The reason there's a pyramid on the Great Seal of the U.S. is that its designer, William Barton, felt that pyramids signify strength and durability.

Look at the back of a $1 bill and you'll notice the pyramid is unfinished. Barton said he designed it that way to show that the country will always grow, improve and build.

What are some classic ironies?

One of the inventors of TV, Philo Farnsworth, never watched TV in his later years and refused to have a TV set in his home because he disapproved of much of the programming.

The rock musician known as Meat Loaf has been a vegetarian for much of his life.

The famous leader of France, Napoleon, was not French at all, but had been born of Italian parents on the island of Corsica.

Likewise, the infamous leader of Germany, Adolph Hitler, was not from Germany. He was born and grew up in Austria.

While filming an action scene in the movie "Troy," in 2004, actor Brad Pitt tore his Achilles tendon. The character he was playing in that movie: Achilles.

Ever wonder how many words we use that are really abbreviations of the original word?

We use the word rehab instead of the original rehabilitation. We say something is out of sync, rarely saying the original word, synchronization.

Memorandum has become memo. Laboratory has become lab. Limousine has become limo. Photograph has become photo. Typographical error has become typo. Veterinarians have become vets. Examination has become exam. Brassiere has become bra.

The words taxi cab came to us from the French taximetre cabriolet. Can you imagine someone today saying, "Call me a taximetre cabriolet." Likewise, the word bus originally came from the longer word, omnibus.

And, in the latest technology world, applications have become apps—not applications.

New York City's population is bigger than the population of how many U.S. states?

The population of New York City is bigger than the population of 39 different U.S. states.

New York City's population is 8.3 million. (That's the population of just the city itself and does not include what is called the metropolitan area which is even bigger). Only 11 states have more than 8.3 million people—California, Texas, Florida, New York, Illinois, Pennsylvania, Ohio, Georgia, Michigan, North Carolina and New Jersey.

The other 39 U.S. states each have populations less than 8.3 million—less population than New York City alone. That's kind of amazing when you stop to think about it. In other words, more people live in New York City than live in the whole state of Massachusetts, or Indiana, or Missouri, or Minnesota, or so many others.

Which 2 women raised in the United States became prime ministers of a foreign nation?

One was Golda Meir who grew up in Milwaukee, graduated from high school there, then at age 23 moved to the land that became Israel, and in 1969 Golda Meir was elected prime minister of Israel.

The other woman who grew up in the U.S. and became prime minister of a foreign nation was Janet Rosenberg from Chicago. She met Cheddi Jagan from the country of Guyana in South America who had come to Chicago to attend college. They soon married and moved to Guyana. There, as Janet Jagan, she got involved in politics and was elected prime minister of Guyana in 1997.

What was controversial about the line just before the intermission in the movie "Gone With the Wind"?

One of the great lines in movie history was in the scene in "Gone With the Wind" when Vivien Leigh, as Scarlett O'Hara, returns to her plantation, Tara, after the Civil War and sees nothing but destruction. The house and grounds are in ruins. She has no money and no food, but she's determined to fight back.

Scarlett pulls a raw turnip caked with mud off the ground, takes a bite, and dramatically says, "As God is my witness, I'll never be hungry again."

Suddenly the screen goes dark and the word "Intermission" appears. When the movie has been shown in theaters, the lights in theaters then come on and it's time for the audience to go to the concessions stands.

There are some movie buffs who have suggested that scene with the line, "I'll never be hungry again," was intentionally placed at the intermission to subliminally get people to go to the concessions stands and get some food.

Is that true? Some say MGM did that to help theater owners. Others say no, that was not thought of when producers were deciding where in the movie to break for the intermission. No one today really knows for sure.

Can the second paragraph below be understood?

Below is an amazing paragraph that shows how the human mind works. Every word of more than three letters is badly misspelled—yet, according to research, as long as the first and last letters of a word are in the right place even though the other letters in the word are mixed up, people can understand each word and the paragraph's meaning. (This has something to do with the reason that speed reading can work, too). Here goes:

I cdnuolt blveiee taht I cluod aulaclty uesdnatnrd waht I was rdanieg. The phaonmneal pweor of the hmuan mnid. Aoccdrnig to a rscheearch at Cmabrigde Uinervtisy, it deosn't mttaer in waht oredr the ltteers in a wrod are. The olny iprmoatnt tihng is taht the frist and lsat ltteer be in the rghit pclae. The rset can be a taotl mses and you can sitll raed it wouthit a porbelm. Tihs is bcuseae the huamn mnid deos not raed ervey lteter by istlef, but the wrod as a wlohe. Amzanig, huh? Yaeh and I awlyas thuohgt slpeling was ipmorantt.

164

Is there really a town in America called Hell?

There is indeed a town named Hell. It's west of Detroit, about 15 miles from Ann Arbor, Mich.

There are several theories on how Hell, Mich., got its name. One is that a German immigrant arrived in the area in the 1830s and said, in German, "So schon hell," which translates to "so beautifully bright." Locals then began calling it by its German name and shortened it to just the last word of "hell." Another theory is that an early settler who had just built a sawmill there was asked by others in the area what he thought the town should be called. "I don't care," he said. "You can name it Hell if you want to."

Two great things about Hell, Mich.: You can really see Hell freeze over. If you go there at the right time when snow and ice are around, you will see Hell freeze over.

And a newspaper reporter on a hot summer day in Detroit, checked the temperatures in Detroit and in Hell, Mich. He found it was hotter in Detroit, so he wrote, "The temperature in Detroit today was hotter than Hell."

Why are tuxedos called tuxedos?

Tobacco millionaire Griswold Lorillard belonged to an exclusive country club outside of New York City in the late 1800s. At the club's annual Autumn Ball in those days, all gentlemen were expected to wear formal black tie and tails. But for the Ball of

1886, Lorillard decided to wear something different.

He had heard that England's fashionable Prince of Wales had just had the tails cut off his formal jacket when he had visited one of the outposts of the British Empire. Lorillard thought that was a good idea and had his own tailor create a tailless black dinner jacket.

When Lorillard wore it to the Ball, it created a stir. Older members thought it was scandalous, but younger members liked this new, more practical formal jacket and soon asked their own tailors to make them the same kind.

Thus was born a new style. The club where all this happened was the Tuxedo Country Club in Tuxedo Park, N.Y.—and the new tailless jacket was named a tuxedo, after the name of the club and the town.

What big innovation happened at a small restaurant—Louis' Lunch—in New Haven, Conn.?

A group of construction workers were working near the Louis' Lunch restaurant in New Haven in 1900. One day they came into Louis' Lunch and asked the proprietor, a man named Louis Lassen, if he could fix them some sandwiches to go, so they could take their food back to their job and eat it there.

Louis Lassen had some hamburger patties cooking on his grill and got the then-revolutionary idea of putting hamburgers into some buns he had so the workers could carry them out.

Thus, the hamburger-on-a-bun as we know it today was born. Before that, hamburger patties were served just as pieces of meat on a plate and not as sandwiches in a bun.

The Library of Congress gives credit to Louis' Lunch as the original creator of the hamburger on a bun.

What's the strange coincidence about the names of assassins?

So many of the assassins of famous people were all known by three-word names.

Among them were John Wilkes Booth who assassinated Abraham Lincoln; Lee Harvey Oswald, the assassin connected with John Kennedy's death; Mark David Chapman who shot a member of the Beatles, John Lennon; and James Earl Ray, the man charged with assassinating Martin Luther King Jr.

What are 7 questions to ponder?

If an orange is called an orange, why isn't a lemon called a yellow?

Why is a boxing ring square, and not round, since it's called a ring?

What do people in China call their good plates—do they call them china?

Why are seats at a ballpark called stands when they're made for sitting?

Why is "abbreviation" such a long word?

Why is the time of day with the slowest traffic called the rush hour?

Do vegetarians eat animal crackers?

Which 4 U.S. state capital cities are named after a U.S. president?

The only four presidents honored with a U.S. state capital city being named after them are Andrew Jackson, Thomas Jefferson, Abraham Lincoln and James Madison.

The capital cities are Jackson, Miss.; Jefferson City, Mo.; Lincoln, Neb.; and Madison, Wisc.

Who was the first singer to have a record that sold 1-million copies?

It wasn't any pop music singer or group.

The first 1-million selling record was made by an opera star, Enrico Caruso.

He recorded "Vesti la Giubba" (Put on the costume) from the opera "Pagliacci" in 1904—and it became the first million-selling record in history.

Which country in the world has 18 letters in its name—and, amazingly, every other letter is a vowel and every other letter is a consonant, all the way through?

That country with the amazing name is a nation on the Arabian Peninsula that has come into prominence in recent years as a tourist and business center with its tall building that's 163 stories high in addition to its shopping mall that's been called the biggest in the world. The country is the United Arab Emirates.

Take a look at that country's name: United Arab Emirates. Start with the first letter of the name, the "U" and every other letter after that is a vowel. The second letter is an "n" and every other letter after that is a consonant. There are other countries that have alternating vowels and consonants in their name but none with as long a name, and with so many letters, as United Arab Emirates.

What was the legendary "Acres of Diamonds" speech—and what university did it found?

A man named Russell Conwell had a speech called "Acres of Diamonds." He gave that one speech in city after city, town after town, all over America, and then in many places overseas. In all, he delivered that same speech over 6,000 times.

The speech told the story of a man who heard about the discovery of a diamond mine in a far-off land, and how much money was being made from it. This man also wanted to find a diamond mine. So, he sold his property and used that money to travel—searching for where diamonds might be buried.

He traveled everywhere in his search for diamonds—but his search proved futile.

Finally, after traveling the world over, his money was gone and he never did find any diamonds.

But meantime, the new owner of his home found diamonds right there. There were acres of diamonds on the property, right in his own backyard. If the original man had only dug in his own backyard, he would have found diamonds.

The moral of the story is that your "diamonds," or those things you want, may not be far from you—they may be right where you are, if you will only "dig" for them. You may not need to look elsewhere for happiness—look within yourself. You can find the riches of life in one's own place. Everyday opportunities to do good are there. Resources for the good things in life may be present right where you are—and, they are within you.

Conwell, a Baptist minister, began giving his Acres of Diamonds speech (and selling his book with that same message) in the 1860s. By 1884 he had made so much money from that speech, he was able to finance the founding of a new university in Philadelphia. He had been minister of the Grace Baptist Temple—so he called his new university, Temple. Today, Temple is a large university, with over 30,000 students, and it's the only university ever founded on the proceeds from one inspiring speech.

Which U.S. presidential election was the biggest upset?

According to many historians, that biggest presidential upset of all time happened in 1948.

Thomas Dewey was considered a sure thing to win the presidency over Harry Truman. Polls showed Dewey with a huge lead all through the campaign. The New York Times editorialized that Dewey's victory was "a foregone conclusion."

Life magazine ran a full-page picture of Dewey a few weeks before the election with a caption that read, "The next president."

And, there's the famous story of the Chicago Tribune being so sure Dewey would win, they printed their early editions election night, before the results were in, with the headline, "Dewey Defeats Truman."

But when the votes were counted, Truman won—and, incredibly, even more surprisingly, it wasn't even close. Truman wound up with 303 electoral votes to only 189 for Dewey.

(For years after that, Truman, with a big smile, loved to show off that Tribune headline).

Which 3 NFL team nicknames are named after a real person?

The Cleveland Browns got their name from their first coach, Paul Brown.

The Buffalo Bills were named after, naturally, the famous 19th century buffalo hunter and showman, William Cody who was known as Buffalo Bill.

And the Kansas City Chiefs are named in honor of Kansas City Mayor Harold Roe Bartle whose nickname was the Chief. He was always called the Chief, and he was instrumental in having owner Lamar Hunt locate the team in Kansas City. Hunt liked Bartle's nickname and also Bartle's guarantee that many season tickets would be sold, so Hunt named his team after the mayor, and they became the Kansas City Chiefs.

How times change: What bitter enemies of the United States are now friends?

It's an oddity of history, and perhaps even a lesson, of how often enemies of nations later become friends.

For example, during the War of 1812, the British not only invaded the United States but tried to burn down the White House. Today, British officials are welcomed with open arms at the White House and the U.S. and British have been close allies for a long time.

In World War II, Germany and Japan fiercely fought the U.S. Now they are friends of the U.S., and Americans buy many German and Japanese products.

The U.S. fought a long, bitter war in Vietnam. Today, Vietnam is a trading partner with the U.S. and American tourists peacefully visit there.

Times do change.

What was the last state east of the Mississippi to be admitted to the Union?

The answer is West Virginia which became a state in 1862.

Which U.S. president was a soldier, a Navy man, a Hall of Fame baseball player, a football star, a member of the Secret Service, and a college professor?

This is a bit of a trick question.

The answer is Ronald Reagan who played all those parts, and more, in the fifty-plus movies he made in his film career.

He played a soldier in "This Is the Army." He was in the Navy in "Hellcats of the Navy." He played Hall of Fame baseball player Grover Cleveland Alexander in "The Winning Team." He was football star George Gipp in "Knute Rockne All American." He played a Secret Service man in "Secret Service of the Air." He was a college professor in "Bedtime For Bonzo."

And those were only a few of the many varied roles Reagan played—but one role in the movies he never played was…being a president.

What unlucky role did the number 13 play in the U.S. space program?

The first space ship to put humans on the moon was Apollo 11 and that plus space ships named Apollo 12, 14, 15, 16 and 17 also all made it to the moon and back with U.S. astronauts—but Apollo 13 never did make it, and superstitious people said Apollo 13 never should have been given the number 13. Here's what happened:

To compound the number 13 on Apollo 13's name, the flight was launched—of all times—at 13:13 military time. (13:13 in military time is 1:13 p.m. in civilian time). But since the space agency goes by military time, the official launch time was indeed, by chance, believe it or not, 13:13. Then, on the second day into the flight to the moon—which, of all days, was April 13—an oxygen tank exploded on board Apollo 13, putting the crew in real danger. That's when the commander of the space ship, James Lovell, made his famous remark, "Houston, we have a problem here."

That loss of oxygen prevented the flight from accomplishing its mission of landing on the moon, and the spacecraft had to return to Earth. Fortunately, the 3-man crew landed safely. That's the only thing that went right on Apollo 13, and many said that number 13 turned out to be a jinx on Apollo 13.

Which U.S. city suffered one of the strangest disasters ever with, of all things, a molasses flood?

It was called "The Great Molasses Flood"—a flood, not of water, but, would you believe, molasses. It sounds funny but it wasn't—with people killed and property destroyed.

This strangest of all floods happened in Boston in 1919 and among its other names, it's been called the "Boston Molasses Disaster."

It was on a January day in 1919 that a huge storage tank of molasses in the North End of Boston exploded. That tank was 50 feet high and held two million gallons of molasses. (Molasses was frequently used as a sweetener for many products in those days). When that big tank burst, a huge wave of molasses moved down the streets of Boston. That wave of molasses was 8 to 15 feet high and it engulfed everything in its way.

A giant wave of sticky stuff sounds like something from a cartoon, but the surging molasses wave was a real, shockingly destructive force.

The wave of molasses moved so quickly and so forcefully that anyone unlucky enough to be in its way didn't stand much of a chance. They were either knocked over and crushed or drowned in the goo. Twenty-one people were unable to get out of its way and were killed. Aside from the fatalities, more than 150 people were injured, many seriously.

Buildings and houses were swept off their foundations. The molasses snapped the support girders of elevated train tracks and sent them crashing to the ground. Property damage was estimated at around $100 million in today's dollars.

There have been all kinds of disasters in the world but never one quite like this, before or since.

What's unusual about these letters in our alphabet— C, D, I, L, M, V and X?

Those letters, when capitalized, are all seven of the Roman numerals.

It's interesting to note that there are only seven Roman numerals—C, D, I, L, M, V and X—and just those seven are able to form so many numbers.

What was the tallest man-made structure in the world for over 4,000 years?

It's surprising that one structure would be the tallest in the world for over 4,000 years, but that's what happened. The most famous pyramid in Egypt, the Pyramid of Giza, built around 2500 B.C., at over 400 feet high, was indeed the tallest man-made structure in the world for over 4,000 years.

No structure anywhere in the world surpassed it in height from around 2500 B.C. until the A.D. 1800s when such things as the Washington Monument, the Cologne Cathedral and the Eiffel Tower were built.

For over 4,000 years that pyramid stood as the tallest structure in the world. That's a long time to hold a record.

Are all ladybugs female?

The answer is no—but that brings up the added question: If there are male ladybugs, which there are (about half of all ladybugs are male), then why are they called ladybugs?

Ladybugs got their name from grateful monks when these insects, male and female, feasted on pests that were destroying the monks' vineyards. When they saved the grapes, the monks named them after Our Lady, the Virgin Mary.

Fruit growers today find ladybugs helpful and often bring them in to save their crops.

What was the great election mystery involving a man named Harold Stassen?

Some historians say this was one of the greatest U.S. election mysteries of all time.

The story begins when Harold Stassen was elected governor of Minnesota at age 31 in 1938. He was called "The Boy Wonder." He was widely popular and was reelected to two more terms. He drew national attention with his performance as governor, and his speeches. He was good looking, smart, considered to have a great mind and pleasing personality. Then, he became a war hero during World War II. He had a reputation as a brilliant thinker (presidents would later use him as an advisor). There were no known negatives about him.

Political experts said he couldn't miss being president some day.

He was an early favorite for the Republican nomination for president in 1948 against Democrat Harry Truman, but he didn't get it, losing out to the older Tom Dewey. But that was no big deal for Stassen. He was only 41 years old then and still had plenty of time to get a presidential nomination.

He tried again to get his party's nomination four years later, in 1952. But this time he had the bad luck of trying to get the nomination over General Dwight Eisenhower who belatedly decided to run for president—and Eisenhower was probably the most popular man in America at that time, after being a leader of the victory in World War II. So, Stassen didn't get that nomination.

And, sadly for Stassen, that started a chain of failures for him. He couldn't get the nomination in 1956 because Eisenhower, a popular president, ran for re-election. And then, Stassen kept trying every four years after that—and never did get the nomination. He eventually became something of a laughing stock—always trying, never winning.

He tried for the Republican presidential nomination NINE times and failed each time. By then, this former "Boy Wonder" had a sad, permanent aura of defeat about him.

His final indignities occurred when he moved to Pennsylvania and tried to get the nomination for governor there. He failed. Finally, he tried to be the mayor of Philadelphia. He failed to get that nomination, too. Historians are still trying to figure out what happened to the once great potential of Harold Stassen.

Women not allowed to wear pants or jeans?

If you don't think times have changed, look at this story we found that was printed in the New York Times in the 1960s:

The headline on the story was, "No Pants Allowed," and the story, in part, said: "Pants, tailored or formal, and the women in them, are being greeted with less than enthusiasm by the men who run many of New York's leading hotels and restaurants.

'I've taken to calling restaurants to see if I'm allowed in,' says Mrs. Nora Jaffe, an abstract painter who believes she looks better in slacks than she does in most dresses.

James Van Bortel, manager of the Top of the Sixes, says 'We have a flat policy against women wearing pants.'

Thomas Clinton, assistant manager of the Plaza Hotel says, 'Pants are pants, and if women wear them they'll be asked to leave."

Hard to believe now, but true then.

Which U.S. state borders the most other states?

Missouri and Tennessee both hold the record for bordering the most other states. Each borders eight states.

Missouri borders Arkansas, Illinois, Iowa, Kansas, Kentucky, Nebraska, Oklahoma and Tennessee.

Tennessee borders Alabama, Arkansas, Georgia, Kentucky, Mississippi, Missouri, North Carolina and Virginia.

What was the single, most important event of the last thousand years?

Veteran newsman Walter Cronkite once said:

"Hundreds of years from now when kids study history, the one event that will stick out as the most significant milestone of the 10th century to the 21st century will have been human's first walk on the moon, and proof that humans can travel and land away from the Earth and safely return."

Hundreds of years from now, of course, landing and walking on other places in space may be commonplace, but the biggest event of the past 1,000 years, according to Cronkite and others, might well have been the first time humans proved they could do it, and that was in July of 1969.

Which U.S. Supreme Court justice led the National Football League in rushing?

Byron (Whizzer) White was on the U.S. Supreme Court from 1962 to 1993, but before that he had been an All-American football player at the University of Colorado and finished second in the Heisman Trophy voting in 1937.

The next year, he led the NFL in rushing, playing for Pittsburgh, and he led the league in rushing again in 1940 with Detroit.

After his football career, he became a lawyer and assistant attorney general, then was appointed to the nation's highest court in 1962, and became the 12th longest serving justice in U.S. Supreme Court history—after leading the NFL in rushing.

In which 2 states have about one-third of all U.S. presidents been born?

It's surprising that about one-third of all U.S. presidents have been born in just two states, but it's true—15 presidents have been born in either Virginia or Ohio.

Eight presidents were born in Virginia—George Washington, Thomas Jefferson, James Madison, James Monroe, William Henry Harrison, John Tyler, Zachary Taylor and Woodrow Wilson, and seven were born in Ohio—Ulysses Grant, Rutherford Hayes, James Garfield, Benjamin Harrison, William McKinley, William Howard Taft and Warren Harding.

Also surprising is that there were three presidents in a row all born in the same state, Virginia—Jefferson, Madison and Monroe, and three presidents in a row all born in the same state, Ohio—Grant, Hayes and Garfield.

The seven presidents from Ohio all served between 1869 and 1921. There were 11 presidents in that period and seven were from Ohio.

What's the longest day of the year? (The answer may be a surprise)

It's often said that the days around the start of summer are the longest days because there's maximum daylight then, but as far as time goes, the longest day of the year is really in November.

The longest day in all states that have Daylight Saving Time is the first Sunday of November, the official end of Daylight Saving

Time. At 2 a.m. on the first Sunday of November, clocks are turned back to 1 a.m.—making that day 25 hours long.

Which country in the world have the most people wanted to come to?

More people have wanted to come to the United States than anywhere else in the world. The proof is that the U.S. has received a larger number of immigrants over the years than any other nation in history.

Following the American Indians who were already here, mass immigration to America began when the original 13 states were settled largely by colonists from the British Isles. Virtually all the Founding Fathers were of English, Irish or Scottish descent. In 1780, over 75 percent of immigrants had come from the British Isles—but that began to change.

As the U.S. was established as a new land of opportunity along with its famous freedoms, immigrants began arriving from elsewhere.

By the mid-1800s, more immigrants came from other northern and western parts of the European continent—Germany, France and Scandinavia. By the late 1800s, the immigration wave shifted, with more coming from eastern and southern Europe—Russia, Poland, Austria-Hungary and Italy. There was also a huge, separate wave from Ireland caused by the potato famine of the 1840s, with hundreds of thousands of Irish emigrating to America.

Meantime, with the building of the West, more immigrants began arriving from China, Japan and other Asian countries. The 1900s began to see large numbers of Hispanic immigrants from places like Puerto Rico, other islands, Central America and Mexico.

The U.S. stands as the only country in the world to receive so many people who wanted to come to America from so many countries over the years.

From which country have the most immigrants come to America in U.S. history? The answer is: Germany. Today there are more Americans of German ancestry than any other.

Who holds the record for getting the longest standing ovation at the Academy Awards?

The man once described as the greatest artist ever to appear on the screen—Charlie Chaplin—returned to Hollywood in 1972 from his years of retirement in Switzerland to receive an honorary Oscar.

Chaplin, then a frail man of 82, stood on stage with tears in his eyes and a smile on his lips. That symbolized the roles he had played so well. In his films, he made people laugh but he also portrayed tenderness and pathos as perhaps no one else ever has.

The audience at the Academy Awards that night kept applauding and cheering Chaplain, giving him the longest standing ovation in Oscar history, as Chaplain looked on with his tears and smiles.

Which holiday is celebrated in the most countries of the world?

The holiday that's celebrated in the most countries is New Year's.

Virtually every country and culture celebrates New Year's at some time during the year.

Dates for New Year's vary in different countries and religions. The Chinese New Year, for instance, begins at the second new moon after the winter solstice. The Muslim New Year is based on the Islamic calendar with the date changing each year. The Jewish New Year, based on their calendar, always falls in September or October. But whenever it is, New Year's is the most celebrated holiday in the world.

Is there really a town in Washington state named George?

Yes, there is, and people who live there can really say they're from George, Washington.

George is a town of about 500 population. It's just off Interstate 90 between Seattle and Spokane, Wash.

To see how much a billion dollars really is, consider this question: How long would it take you to count a billion dollars?

The government spends a billion dollars here, a billion dollars there—but to realize how much a billion dollars is, look at this: If you wanted to count one billion dollars—one dollar at a time—it would take you 31 years and 251 days if you counted one dollar every second, every day, day and night, day after day, year after year, without stopping.

That's true because 31 years plus 251 days is composed of one billion seconds.

If you wanted to count, say, 10 billion dollars one dollar at a time, you couldn't do it in your lifetime.

As U.S. Senator Everett Dirksen once said, "You spend a billion dollars here and a billion dollars there, and pretty soon you're talking about real money."

How incredibly crowded is the country of Bangladesh?

Although Bangladesh is a very small country, it has the eighth largest population in the world—and here's the really incredible fact:

The whole country of Bangladesh is about the same size as the U.S. state of Iowa—but while Iowa has about 3 million people, Bangladesh has over 160 million people. That's crowded.

It's also amazing to learn that Russia, the largest country in the world in area—100 times bigger than Bangladesh—has fewer people than Bangladesh does.

The Chicago Bears of the NFL once beat the Washington Redskins 73-0—and aside from that big score, what was an oddity about that game?

In addition to that game setting the record at the time for the most points ever scored by one team in one NFL game, the oddity is this: This was not just another game. It was the championship game of the league in that season of 1940, supposedly played by the two best teams in the league, facing each other. Yet one team—the Bears—were able to score a record-breaking 73 points against their opponent and beat them 73-0.

One other little oddity is that in those days officials didn't have as many footballs on hand as they do today and there were no nets to prevent extra-point kicks and field goals from going into the stands. By the time the fourth quarter started, officials began to run out of footballs and so they asked the Bears not to kick any more extra points or field goals, and to just run or pass the ball instead.

Which U.S. state has the exact same name as a foreign country?

The answer is Georgia.

The country of Georgia is located in Southwest Asia, bordering on Russia, Turkey, Armenia, Azerbaijan and the Black Sea. It was originally called Gorj, the name of early settlers there in B.C. times. Over the centuries, the country was occupied by Turks, Mongols, Greeks and Persians and the name of the country evolved from Gorj to Georgia. Today, the country of Georgia uses as its national flag, the flag of its patron saint, St. George, with its five crosses.

Meantime, the U.S. state of Georgia got its name in an entirely different way. It was named after King George II of England.

What well-known, highly rated university in America is named after a teenager?

It's Stanford University in Palo Alto, Calif.

Shortly after 15-year-old Leland Stanford Jr. died of typhoid fever in 1884, his father, Leland Stanford, a railroad tycoon and former governor and U.S. senator from California, gave money to establish a university to honor his son's memory.

Stanford University is thus the only major university in the U.S. named after a teenage boy.

In how many countries do people drive on the left?

There are a surprisingly large number of countries where you have to drive on the left. Driving on the left is the law in more than one-fourth of all the nations of the world—52 out of 196.

Driving on the left, of course, is the law in Great Britain—and in almost all the many old British colonies around the world. The two major exceptions are the former British colonies of the United States and Canada.

Driving on the left is still the rule in the ex-British colonies of Australia, New Zealand, India, Pakistan, Bangladesh, the Bahamas, Fiji, Jamaica, Kenya, Singapore, South Africa and many more.

A big surprise is a major country that had nothing to do with Britain, and was never a British colony, but today has driving on the left, and that is Japan. Many tourists are surprised when they get to Japan and see driving on the left.

Another surprise is that there is a land under United States control that has driving on the left. That is the U.S. Virgin Islands. The reason it has driving on the left is that the majority of the Virgin Islands (six of the nine main islands) are the British Virgin Islands and for consistency sake, the remaining three main islands, which the U.S. acquired in 1917, kept the old British custom of driving on the left to avoid confusion with the rest of the Virgin Islands.

How can birds and fish know how to travel to exact locations?

One of the intriguing mysteries of nature is that while so-called intelligent humans need maps, compasses, GPS systems or directions to find their way, fish like salmon can swim 1,000 miles or more through dark ocean depths (with no signposts) and get back to the exact fresh-water stream where they were born as they return to their birth site to mate to make a new generation—and migrating birds can fly hundreds or thousands of miles back to the exact spot from which they started, like the swallows returning to Capistrano, Calif., each year from South America. How do they do it?

Scientists don't know the answer. They point out that birds, for instance, can fly over oceans and lakes in bad, cloudy weather when they can't be guided by the sun or stars or landmarks, and yet still reach their destination.

Incredibly, those birds, and fish know where they're going. The only answer most scientists can come up with is that a "compass" is somehow programmed in their genes—a wonder of nature.

How can a baseball pitcher be credited with a win without ever throwing a pitch to a batter?

A relief pitcher enters the game in the top of the ninth inning in a tie game with two outs and a runner on first base. The pitcher then picks the runner off first base for the third out without pitching to a batter. The pitcher's team scores a run in the bottom of the ninth to win the game and that relief pitcher gets credit as the winning pitcher.

How is Easter's date figured?

Ever wonder how the date for Easter is determined each year?

Easter is always the first Sunday after the first full moon of spring.

That means Easter can never be earlier than March 22, and it can never be later than April 25.

Who was the only person who was both the chief justice of the U.S. Supreme Court AND president of the United States?

After William Howard Taft suffered his embarrassing defeat when he ran for a second term as U.S. president in 1912 and finished third in the voting, he left politics and went back to his alma mater, Yale, to teach in their law school.

But nine years after his bad presidential defeat, he was back in the national spotlight when President Warren Harding chose Taft to be chief justice of the U.S. Supreme Court. Taft served as chief justice from 1921 until his death in 1930.

Taft became the only person in U.S. history to have been both president and chief justice. During his years on the Supreme Court, he, perhaps not surprisingly, said he enjoyed being chief justice much more than being president.

What's the longest word in the English language that never uses the same letter twice?

The longest word we can find with no letter repeated is a 15-letter word: uncopyrightable.

Why are hot dogs called hot dogs?

Hot dogs got their name at a baseball game in New York in the early 1900s.

It was a cool day at the game that day, and looking for something warm to sell, concessionaire Harry Stevens went to a neighborhood butcher shop and was ready to buy a supply of warm sausages to serve the fans, but wondered how the fans could hold them. The butcher said there was a bakery next door, so Stevens went there and bought some buns to hold the sausages. The hot dog was born—but it didn't have a name yet.

A New York newspaper cartoonist, Tad Dorgan, was at the game that day and saw vendors selling sausages in buns. The sausages reminded him of a dachshund, so he drew a cartoon of a dachshund in a bun and was going to title his cartoon "Hot Dachshund." But then he wasn't sure how to spell dachshund, so he settled for "Hot Dog," and a new name was created.

Dorgan's historic cartoon that gave hot dogs their name is on display today at the baseball Hall of Fame in Cooperstown, N.Y.

How have computers changed our language?

Before the computer age, a mouse was an animal.

The web was something a spider made.

A program was something on radio or TV.

A cursor was a person who swore.

A virus was an illness.

An app or application was something you made for employment.

And a hard drive was a long trip on the road.

Where was the deadliest fire in U.S. history?

Many Americans have heard about the famous Chicago fire that supposedly was started when Mrs. O'Leary's cow kicked over a lighted lantern in 1871. That was a memorable fire and is in the history books and U.S. lore—BUT it can't compare with another fire that, strangely enough, happened at exactly the same time somewhere else.

The Chicago fire was bad enough. It destroyed a lot of buildings in a 3-square mile area and took the lives of about 300 people, but look what happened more than 200 miles north of Chicago on that same night:

Around the little town of Peshtigo, Wisc., 45 miles northeast of Green Bay, a raging forest fire spread and spread. That Peshtigo forest fire, which started on Oct. 8, 1871, the same night as the Chicago fire far away, eventually wiped out 3.8 million acres of forest and farmland, and more significantly, resulted in more deaths than have ever been caused by any other single fire in the nation. The death toll from the Peshtigo fire reached a total of almost 2,000 people.

Oddly, history little remembers the Peshtigo fire, but in terms of deaths and destruction, it holds the record as the worst disaster caused by fire alone in U.S. history.

What's the only non-Ivy League college that produced 3 U.S. presidents?

The only non-Ivy League college that has produced three U.S. presidents is William & Mary in Williamsburg, Va.

The three presidents who went to William & Mary were Thomas Jefferson, James Monroe and John Tyler.

What's been the longest-running show in America?

It's a circus—the Ringling Brothers and Barnum & Bailey Circus, and here's the story about it.

It was all started by one of the world's great showmen, Phineas T. Barnum. While putting on various shows and circuses in the mid-1800s, he coined the phrase, "The Greatest Show on Earth". Barnum eventually took in a partner, James Bailey—and that created the Barnum & Bailey name. Then in the early 1900s, the Ringling Brothers bought the Barnum & Bailey circus, combined it with theirs, and added their name. That gave this long-running circus its really long name—the Ringling Brothers and Barnum & Bailey Circus.

There were five Ringling brothers, Albert, Otto, Alfred, Charles and John. As they grew up in Baraboo, Wisc., they began giving shows doing juggling acts, singing songs and acting as clowns. By 1884, they saved enough money to start a wagon show with a trained horse and a dancing bear. Four years later, they bought their first elephant, and by 1890, they had a full-fledged circus, traveling from town to town.

The combined Ringling Brothers and Barnum & Bailey Circus lasted over 100 years, before ending in 2017, and thus holds the record as the longest running continuous show in American history.

How could a person be 15 years old in 1985 and then, truthfully, be only 10 years old in 1990?

How's that possible?

It could have happened in B.C. times when years were figured in descending order, and 1985 came after 1990.

What 2 countries had exactly the same flag—and didn't know it?

Haiti and Liechtenstein had the same flag but weren't aware of it until they got to the Olympics for the first time and saw each other's flag.

The flags were identical with solid blue on the top half and solid red on the bottom half.

After the Olympics, they each went home and made minor changes to make their flags different. Haiti added a coat of arms in the middle of their flag, and Liechtenstein added a gold crown in the upper left-hand corner of their flag. And that's the way they are today.

What is unique about this sentence?

Dennis, Nell, Edna, Leon, Anita, Rolf, Nora, Alice, Carol, Leo, Jane, Reed, Dena, Dale, Basil, Rae, Penny, Lana, Dave, Denny, Lena, Ida, Bernadette, Ben, Ray, Lila, Nina, Jo, Ira, Mara, Sara, Mario, Jan, Ina, Lily, Arne, Bette, Dan, Reba, Diane, Lynn, Ed, Eva, Dana, Lynne, Pearl, Isabel, Ada, Ned, Dee, Rena, Joel, Lora, Cecil, Aaron, Flora, Tina, Noel and Ellen sinned.

It's one of the most amazing sentences ever written: This whole, long sentence is a palindrome—a sentence that reads the same backward or forward. Usually palindromes are short sentences, like: "Able was I ere I saw Elba," but this classic is a long one.

Which U.S. first lady was just 21 years old?

Here's how the U.S. once had a first lady who was just 21.

It came about when Grover Cleveland was elected president in 1884. He was a bachelor when elected, but after about a year in office, he married 21-year-old Frances Folsom who had been his ward since her father had died when she was 9 years old. Her father had been Cleveland's former law partner.

At age 21, Frances Folsom Cleveland became the youngest first lady in U.S. history. President Cleveland was 49 at the time.

The U.S. has also had one other first lady in her twenties. President John Tyler's first wife died and Tyler married 24-year-old Julia Gardiner three years into his presidency in 1844. Tyler was 54.

In case you're wondering, Jackie Kennedy, wife of President John Kennedy, was 31 when she became first lady in 1961. President Kennedy was 43 at the time, and Jackie Kennedy became the third-youngest U.S. first lady.

What's odd about the names San Juan and Puerto Rico?

As you know, San Juan is the capital and biggest city of Puerto Rico—but the oddity is that the city of San Juan used to be known as Puerto Rico and the island itself used to be called San Juan—and they completely switched names.

It figures the city would be called Puerto Rico because that means "rich port" in Spanish, so that was the original name Spanish explorers gave the city—Puerto Rico, and they called the whole island San Juan.

But over time, people began reversing the names and calling the island Puerto Rico and the city San Juan, and that's the way it is today, exactly the opposite of the names they used to have.

What are the odds that in any group of 23 people, 2 will have the same birthday?

This is a story from statistical experts that's hard to believe, but they say it's true.

Suppose, for example, you are at a party with 22 strangers and, while talking with one, you discover that your birthday date and month is the same as his. A remarkable coincidence? No. The odds, say statisticians, are better than 50-50 that in any group of 23 people chosen at random, at least two will have identical birthdays.

We tried that one night on our radio show. We asked listeners to call in and give their birth dates. To make this test legitimate, we asked listeners to give the date and month of their birth just to our producer off the air so that no one could ruin the survey by mischievously copying someone else's answer. The producer, using our call screen, also made sure the same person wasn't calling twice

Wouldn't you know, it worked. Two of the first 23 callers, at random, had the same birthday. Try it yourself on the next 22 people you talk to, and see if any have the same birthday as you.

What was unusual about the names of Americans in the early days of the nation?

Just about everybody today has a middle name, but, surprisingly, in the early days of the nation, very few people had middle names.

For example, George Washington had no middle name, and none of the first five U.S. presidents had middle names. Besides Washington, there were John Adams, Thomas Jefferson, James Madison and James Monroe. Those were their full names.

The first president with a middle name was the sixth president, John Quincy Adams, but then he was followed by Andrew Jackson with no middle name, and for many more years, most of the presidents—and the general population—had no middle names. Abraham Lincoln had no middle name.

The custom didn't begin to change until the late 1800s when most parents began giving their children middle names.

Why is basketball in the Summer Olympics and not the Winter Olympics even though basketball is mostly a winter sport—played in winter months?

The Olympics have a little rule that prevents basketball from being played at the Winter Olympics.

That rule says all sports in the Winter Olympics must be contested on…ice or snow, so it's that Olympic ice or snow rule that keeps basketball from being played in its natural time of the Winter Olympics, and moves basketball, as far as the Olympics are concerned, from winter-time to the Summer Olympics.

What was not-so-super about the lives of the boys who created Superman?

Two high school kids in Cleveland, Jerry Siegel and Joe Shuster, dreamed up Superman in the 1930s, and created the first pictures and story of Superman.

In March, 1938, they sold the rights to Superman for $130. When Superman proved to be an immediate sensation, Siegel and Shuster tried to get a share of the profits. They were turned down—and spent most of the rest of their lives in near poverty.

The Superman brand has earned more than $1 billion in movies, books, TV, and commercial products. Meanwhile, Siegel and Shuster as adults had trouble making a living.

Late in life, they finally did receive a $20,000 annuity. Shuster, then blind, died in 1992. Siegel, in an interview before his death in 1996, said, "I can't stand to look at Superman. It makes me physically ill." Not a super life for the creators of Superman.

What's the biggest state east of the Mississippi?

Most of the biggest states in area in the U.S. are west of the Mississippi River. In fact, the 20 biggest states in the nation are all west of the Mississippi, led by Alaska, Texas and California.

The biggest state east of the Mississippi based on land area, is Georgia, followed by Michigan and Florida.

How did the U.S. get valuable intelligence in World War II from a mediocre baseball player?

This story involves a second-string major league baseball catcher by the name of Moe Berg. In his undistinguished big league career from 1923 to 1939, Berg averaged just about 40 games a season, had a lifetime batting average under .250, and hit just six home runs in his 15 years.

Although he wasn't a great ballplayer, he was a highly educated fellow who could speak eight languages. The joke around baseball was that he couldn't hit in any language.

Meantime, in 1934, a group of major league baseball all-stars was picked for a post-season tour of Japan. The Japanese were becoming increasingly interested in baseball, organizing their own leagues, and were eager to have America's best players come to their country and show 'em how it was done in the big leagues of America.

On the 1934 all-star baseball team the U.S. was going to show off to the Japanese were many of the top players of the time, including the great Babe Ruth and Lou Gehrig. But also on that all-star team was that obscure non-star, Moe Berg.

Apparently, the Japanese, with their lack of a lot of knowledge about American baseball then, didn't question why Berg was on the all-star team, and there's no evidence they had any suspicions about why Berg was there.

Berg was there as a U.S paid spy. In Japan, in the afternoons of the night baseball games, Berg, with his ability to speak Japanese, freely moved around Tokyo and other cities, dressed in a kimono. Under that kimono was a hidden camera. Berg took as many pictures as he could. The most significant occurred one day when he went to a Tokyo hospital, ostensibly to take flowers to the daughter of an America diplomat being treated there. Once inside the hospital, Berg snuck up to the roof, which had a magnificent, clear, miles-wide view. The pictures Berg took from that vantage point, and others he took around Japan, gave the U.S. valuable intelligence that would be instrumental in the success of the bombing of Tokyo and other Japanese cities in World War II.

After the war, the story of Berg's spy work was released publicly, and there was a book about Berg, titled "The Catcher was a Spy." Moe Berg goes down in history, certainly not as a great ballplayer, but as a great U.S. spy.

What expressions use the name of an animal to describe a human situation?

Ever realize how many expressions we use to describe a human situation that are named after animals—in fact, almost any animal you can think of is used to describe one human situation or another. Here are some, and perhaps you can enjoy thinking of more:

Dog tired, wise as an owl, busy as a beaver, gentle as a lamb, stubborn as a mule, crocodile tears, strong as an ox, going at a snail's pace, eating crow, playing possum, pigeon toed, take the bull by the horns, puppy love, an elephant in the room, butterflies in the stomach, pig out, a cat nap, like a fish out of water, a fly in the ointment, sheepish, I have a frog in my throat, slippery as an eel, he has a tiger by the tail.

And those are only the beginning. What more can you think of?

Which U.S. president came up with an advertising slogan that's still used for a product today?

When Theodore Roosevelt was president in the early 1900s, he visited the Maxwell House Hotel in Nashville, Tenn., and was served a specialty of the house, their special brand of coffee.

When the hotel manager asked Roosevelt what he thought of the coffee, Roosevelt said, "It's good to the last drop." A few years later when the coffee began to be marketed nationally, they used his quote as their slogan (and still do).

It became one of the best-known and longest-lasting slogans of all time. (But some jokesters have asked what's wrong with the last drop).

Who are some famous people who lived to 100 years of age or more?

Songwriter Irving Berlin.

Entertainers Bob Hope and George Burns.

Rose Kennedy, the mother of U.S. President John Kennedy.

Louisiana governor Jimmy Davis who was also a song writer and wrote "You Are My Sunshine."

Football coach Amos Alonzo Stagg.

U.S. Senator Strom Thurmond.

Painter Grandma Moses.

Why do we hang stockings at Christmas time?

According to legend, the custom goes back to the fourth century with the real St. Nicholas, who lived in what is now Turkey, and was famous for giving gifts and money.

Nicholas was from a wealthy family and heard about three poor girls whose family was impoverished. Each night, the girls would wash the one pair of stockings each had, and hang them by the fireplace to dry.

One Christmas Eve, Nicholas entered their house after they had gone to bed and put gold coins in their stockings.

That magical appearance of those gifts became known throughout the town, and then other people began hanging stockings in hopes of similar good luck. The custom spread and a tradition was born.

In 1822, Clement Clarke Moore wrote about it in his famous poem, " 'Twas the Night Before Christmas," when he said, "The stockings were hung by the chimney with care, in hopes that St. Nicholas soon would be there." And the custom continues.

Why are the Christmas colors red and green?

Christmas colors became red and green from the fact that early Christmas tree decorations consisted of red apples on the green tree.

Space firsts: Who was the first person in space, the first Americans in space, and the first women in space?

The first human ever to fly in space was Yuri Gagarin of the Soviet Union with a 1-hour, 48- minute orbital flight on April 12, 1961.

First American in space was Alan Shepard with a 15- minute non-orbital flight on May 5, 1961.

First American in orbit was future U.S. Senator John Glenn with a 4-hour, 55 minute flight that orbited the Earth three times, on Feb. 20, 1962. (That prompted President John Kennedy to challenge the U.S. to get to the moon in that decade, which the U.S. did).

First woman in space was Valentina Tereshkova of the Soviet Union with a 70-hour flight on June 16, 1963.

First American woman in space was Sally Ride, a crew member on the space shuttle Challenger on a 6-day flight beginning June 18, 1983.

(Despite the Russians early lead in space flight, only Americans— 12 in all—have ever walked on the moon, beginning with Neil Armstrong and Buzz Aldrin on July 20, 1969).

How is it possible that the first winner of the Miss America pageant was not from any of the 50 U.S. states?

The Miss America pageant began in 1921, and the first winner was Margaret Gorman who was not from any of the 50 states. She was from Washington, D.C.

George Washington lived in the White House 30 years BEFORE he was president—how's that possible?

When Washington married a rich Virginia widow, Martha Custis, her big home, by coincidence, was known as the "White House." Washington lived there with Martha in 1759, 30 years before he became president.

As it turned out, the place we know today as the White House—the president's house—wasn't completed during Washington's terms as president, and he became the only president who never lived in the presidential White House—but he did live in another White House, with his wife, Martha.

Where's the deepest lake in the United States?

No, it's not one of the Great Lakes.

Deepest lake in the U.S. is Crater Lake in Oregon. It's about 2,000 feet deep and was formed in the crater of an old volcano in the Cascade Mountains.

Aside from its depth, it's known for its beautiful, clear water.

How long did it take for women anywhere in the world to get the right to vote in a national election?

It seems incredible now, but no woman—in any country—was allowed to vote in a national election until New Zealand became the first nation to give women the vote, in 1893.

Once New Zealand did that, other countries followed—but slowly.

Australia was next, in 1902.   Then came some European countries. The U.S. gave women the vote in national elections for the first time, in 1920.

There are 196 countries in the world, yet only 4 of them have just a one-syllable name. Which countries are those?

You'd think there would be more, but there are only four countries with a one-syllable name—and those four countries are Chad, France, Greece and Spain.

That's all there are, and oddly enough, two of them are neighboring countries, France and Spain.

The 67 highest mountains in the world are all in Asia, led by Mt. Everest whose height is 29,035 feet —but where's the highest mountain not in Asia?

The highest mountain outside of Asia is in Argentina, in South America. It's Mt. Aconcagua whose height is 22,831 feet.

Highest mountain in North America is Mt. Denali in Alaska (formerly known as Mt. McKinley), at 20,320 feet. Highest in Africa is Mt. Kilimanjaro in Tanzania at 19,341 feet, and the highest mountain solely in Europe is Mont Blanc, which borders France and Italy in the Alps, and stands 15,781feet high.

Who's the only person ever elected to a high government office who had also walked on the moon?

Only 12 humans—all Americans—have ever walked on the moon, and of those 12, only one was ever elected to a high government office.

That was astronaut Harrison Schmitt who walked on the moon in 1972 and was elected to the U.S. Senate from his home state of New Mexico. He served in the Senate from 1977 to 1983.

You might think of astronaut John Glenn who was elected to the Senate from Ohio—but Glenn, who made several flights into space, never made it to the moon.

Which 2 U.S. presidents were so popular, nobody ran against them?

George Washington was one of those two presidents. When he ran for both his terms, he had no opponent. He got all the electoral votes, becoming the only president elected unanimously.

Then in 1820 when James Monroe ran for his second term, things were so good in the country, it was called the Era of Good Feeling, and nobody ran against him. Monroe got all electoral votes except one—one elector voted for somebody else, not because he was against Monroe, but just because he said he wanted Washington to be the only president elected unanimously—but Monroe still won with nobody running against him.

It's unlikely that will ever happen again. Those days are gone.

Although Connie Mack was a big league baseball manager longer than anyone else—50 years—he was not allowed to go onto the field during a game to argue with an umpire or change pitchers. Why not?

Mack didn't wear a uniform when he was a manager. He sat in the dugout wearing street clothes—a suit and tie.

Major League baseball rules say anyone who goes on the field during a game, except grounds keepers and medical staff, must be in uniform, so Mack was not able to go out on the field to argue with an umpire or talk to, or change, pitchers.

Why are they called VICE presidents? (Did they do something wrong?)

Our usual meaning of the word "vice" has to do with corruption or crime—but that's not why U.S. vice presidents and other vice presidents got that title.

The use of vice in the title of vice president comes from an old Scottish meaning of the word vice. The old Scots used the word vice as a synonym for "alternate" or "substitute," and that definition of vice was used in our language many years ago.

That's how our vice presidents came to be called vice presidents today, meaning alternate or substitute or next in command.

What movie star died at age 14 but left a son who also made movies?

He was the most popular movie star of 1926, according to a poll of theater owners that year.

He was...a dog named Rin Tin Tin—and he was so popular he was often billed above human actors in his films.

Rin Tin Tin appeared in some 15 movies before his death at age 14, in 1932. And then his son, Rin Tin Tin Jr., succeeded him in several films through the 1930s.

Rin Tin Tin starred in such movies as "Jaws of Steel," The Night Cry," and "A Dog of the Regiment."

Ever realize how many things are misnamed?

French fries did not originate in France. They originated in Belgium, but then the French began making them and when French immigrants brought them to America, they began to be called French fries.

The coins we call nickels originally were made of all nickel, but today they are made of 75 percent copper and only 25 percent nickel. Perhaps we should call them coppers instead of nickels.

A ten-gallon hat does not hold 10 gallons. It holds only about three-quarters of a gallon. The use of the word gallon here comes from the Spanish word "galon," which is the name for the braid used to decorate the hats. It has nothing to do with liquid measure. Ten pieces of Spanish braids decorated the original ten-gallon hats.

Russian dressing did not come from Russia. It was first made in America.

Likewise, English muffins did not originate in England but in the U.S.

The famous Oktoberfest in Munich, Germany, doesn't begin in October. It's a two-week celebration that begins in September and only the final few days are in October.

The Battle of Bunker Hill in the American Revolutionary War did not take place on Bunker Hill. It was fought on nearby Breed's Hill in Boston. The commander of troops that day had orders to protect Bunker Hill, and he chose to fight the battle on nearby Breed's Hill.

Catgut, used in musical instruments, doesn't come from cats but from intestines of sheep.

Venetian blinds did not originate with the Venetians in Venice, Italy. They were invented by the Japanese. Maybe they should be called Japanese blinds.

The musical instrument called the English horn is not a horn and it's not English. It's an oboe that was really developed in France.

In Shakespeare's play, "A Midsummer Night's Dream," the action does not take place in midsummer, but in the spring, around May Day.

Which human body parts have just 3 letters in their name?

Here are 10 human body parts with 3-letter names:

Arm
Ear
Eye
Gum
Hip
Jaw
Leg
Lip
Rib
Toe

It took a long time, but who was the first U.S. president born in a hospital?

It seems hard to believe, but Jimmy Carter, president from 1977 to 1981, was the very first U.S. president to be born in a hospital.

Carter was born in 1924. All previous presidents were born at home. That was the custom well into the 20th century.

Why is the emergency phone number 9-1-1?

When the 9-1-1 emergency phone number was put into use in the 1960s, it was originally going to be 9-9-9, but was changed for a very good reason, and, interestingly, the name that people used to refer to 9-1-1 was changed, too.

First, the reason it was changed from the original 9-9-9 to 9-1-1 was that many people had rotary dial phones in those days, and 9 took longer to dial than 1. Phone companies had to keep the first 9 for technical reasons, but they changed the last two digits to 1 and made it 9-1-1 for faster dialing.

And, the other change: When the switch was made to 9-1-1, it was called 9-eleven, but some people complained there was no eleven on their phones, so the name was changed from 9-eleven to 9-one-one to be perfectly clear.

What's the appropriate name for the basketball court in the U.S. Supreme Court building in Washington?

In the U.S. Supreme Court building in Washington, there are five floors, and on the top floor, there's a gym for use by the justices and their clerks and staff.

Part of that gym includes a basketball court which has been given a very appropriate name. That basketball court on the top floor of the Supreme Court building has been called "The highest court in the land."

What was the claim to fame of brothers Maurice and Richard McDonald?

Maurice and Richard McDonald opened a little hamburger stand in San Bernardino, Calif., in 1948. Who could have imagined what would happen next.

There was one man who could—Ray Kroc of Chicago. Kroc was part owner of a milkshake-maker called the Multimixer. He heard that the McDonalds had bought eight Multimixers and wondered how such a small business would have need for so many shake-makers.

Kroc paid a visit to Maurice and Richard's stand one day and was impressed with the way they were selling burgers and shakes in a fast-paced assembly line operation. Inspired, Kroc suggested they open other hamburger stands together, but the McDonald brothers weren't interested.

Undeterred, Kroc decided to buy out Maurice and Richard, which he did. He kept their last name and went on to sell billions of burgers across the country, and then around the world, under the name of the McDonalds.

Which U.S. towns have the same name as a foreign country?

Here are some such towns:

There's Brazil, Ind., Columbia, Mo., Jamaica, N.Y., Lebanon, Pa., Mexico, Mo., Panama City, Fla., Peru, Ind., and Poland, Maine.

How could a person win a U.S. presidential election even if NOBODY voted for him or her in 39 of the 50 states?

Incredibly, a person could indeed win a U.S. presidential election even if nobody voted for him or her in 39 of the 50 states.

It's hard-to-believe, but true, that if a presidential candidate carries just the 11 most populous states—the 11 states with the most Electoral College votes—he or she would have the necessary 270 electoral votes needed to win. Those 11 states are California, Texas, Florida, New York, Illinois, Pennsylvania, Ohio, Georgia, Michigan, North Carolina and New Jersey.

It wouldn't matter what happened in the other 39 states. If nobody voted for that candidate in any of the other 39 states, the candidate would still win the presidency as long as he or she carried the 11 most populous states. Those 11 states have enough combined electoral votes to give a candidate the victory. It's an oddity of the U.S. Electoral College system.

What's the loudest noise ever heard by humans?

Surprisingly, the loudest known explosion in human history was not a nuclear bomb, but an event that happened in 1883—and it was loud.

An 18-square-mile volcanic island named Krakatoa in the South Pacific blew up.The volcano explosion was so big that dust and dirt from the island settled in many parts of the world, and the explosion was so loud, it could be heard 3,000 miles away.

That would be like an explosion in New York being heard in California.

That explosion of the island of Krakatoa ranks as the loudest known noise humans have ever heard.

Why do we eat turkey on Thanksgiving—why turkey?

Would you believe at the first Thanksgiving dinners with the Pilgrims, they did NOT eat turkey, according to many historians today.

Historians say it's more likely the Pilgrims at those first Thanksgivings ate venison, goose, duck and fish.

So, why do we eat turkey today?

The idea of turkey at Thanksgiving began in the 1860s when President Abraham Lincoln was the first president to declare Thanksgiving a regular, annual national holiday. Turkey gradually became the traditional Thanksgiving fare, helped by the abundance of turkeys then in many parts of America, and the custom at that time of cooking turkeys for special occasions.

What famous composer had 20 children?

One of the most famous composers of all time, Johann Sebastian Bach, who lived from 1685 to 1750, had 20 children. He had seven with his first wife and a few years after her death, he married a woman 17 years his junior and they had 13 children together.

Bach was prolific in many ways. Supporting his large family, he served as a musician, a conductor and composed hundreds of compositions, many of which live on today.

Of Bach's 20 children, several became significant musicians themselves.

Before there were airplanes, what's the fastest anyone ever went around the world?

There was a woman named Elizabeth Cochran who got a job with a New York newspaper in the 1800s. Following Jules Verne's fictional story, "Around the World in 80 Days," which was published in 1873, Cochran convinced her editor to let her do a story about trying to go around the world, in reality, in fewer than 80 days.

Under the pen name of Nellie Bly, she did just that, going around the world by boats and trains in 72 days, 6 hours and 11 minutes.

The nation was captivated by her daily stories during the journey, as she beat Verne's 80 days, and set the documented record for going around the world faster than anyone else ever had up to that time.

Which 2 U.S. state capital cities are named after the same person?

The capital city of Ohio, Columbus, and the capital city of South Carolina, Columbia, are both named after Christopher Columbus. (The word "Columbia" is a poetic version of Columbus' name).

Columbus, Ohio and Columbia, S.C., are also the only two U.S. state capital cities that start with the same six letters.

Why is a donkey the symbol for the Democrats, and an elephant the symbol for Republicans?

Those symbols were both popularized by an influential political cartoonist of the 1800s, Thomas Nast.

During one election, Nast drew a cartoon of an elephant representing the Republicans stomping on the planks of the Democrats. Republicans liked that so much, they began using an elephant as their symbol from then on.

As for the donkey and the Democrats, Nast also popularized that. One of his cartoons in another election showed a donkey, representing the Democrats, kicking up its heels in victory. Democrats, pleased with that, then began using the donkey as their symbol.

Why is there a hole in doughnuts?

Originally, doughnuts had no hole in the center.

But along came Hanson Gregory, a sea captain from Rockport, Maine. He's honored as the man who put that distinctive hole in doughnuts—and he did it for a very practical reason.

Gregory loved to eat doughnuts while piloting his ship—and instead of having the doughnuts slide all around while the ship was going through rough waters, he put a hole in his doughnuts so he could place them on a spike near his steering wheel.

Other nearby sailors picked up the idea and the hole in the center of doughnuts gradually became a tradition. Today, there's a plaque in Rockport, Maine, honoring native son Hanson Gregory—as the man who put the hole in doughnuts.

Which U.S. president died on the floor of Congress?

The sixth U.S. president, John Quincy Adams, ran for Congress after he was president and was elected to the House of Representatives. He was then re-elected to the House seven times.

During what turned out to be his final term, in 1848, he was giving a speech on the floor of Congress when he suddenly collapsed and fell to the floor. He had suffered a stroke and was carried to the Speaker's Room at the rear of the chamber where he died—the only president ever to die on the floor of Congress.

What are the only 2 states that touch the Atlantic Ocean that were not one of the original 13 U.S. states?

Florida and Maine which touch the Atlantic were not among the original 13 states.

Florida didn't join the Union until 1845, as the 27th state.

Maine became the 23rd state, joining the Union in 1820.

What was the not-so-joyous U.S. holiday called the Bank Holiday?

President Franklin Roosevelt ordered all banks in the country to be closed, beginning on March 6, 1933, in the midst of the Great

Depression, to help stop the money panic that was sweeping the nation. Depositors had been withdrawing their funds with such speed that many banks were running out of cash, and failing.

A week later, on March 13, only banks that could prove they had enough money were allowed to begin to re-open.

That period when all banks were closed was officially called the "Bank Holiday." That was one holiday that people were glad to see end.

What famous person in history had the same last name as the name of a sport that we have today?

There was an Italian traveler who became famous for his journeys to China and other parts of Asia in the 13th century. The stories of his trips gave Europe the first real information about the Orient. That man had the same name as today's sport of polo. He was Marco Polo.

Among other things, Marco Polo brought Chinese noodles back to Italy, which Italians famously turned into spaghetti, and then introduced it to the world.

Which animals have the longest pregnancies?

Elephants hold the record.

Female elephants are pregnant for as long as 20 months to two years before giving birth to a baby elephant.

What was the original name of "The Star-Spangled Banner"?

When Francis Scott Key wrote the words to "The Star-Spangled Banner" in 1814, he didn't call it that at all.

Key named it "The Defense of Ft. McHenry." Only later was its name changed.

And the music also had a different name. The music for "The Star-Spangled Banner" was taken from an old English drinking song called, "To Anacreon in Heaven."

What are 9 more questions to ponder?

Why does a round pizza come in a square box?

Why is there no pine or apples in pineapples?

Why do people who sleep well say they "slept like a baby" when babies wake up and cry every few hours?

Why is it called quicksand when it works very slowly?

Why are you IN a movie, but ON TV?

Why do they call one TV set a set when it's only one?

Why is it called "after dark" when it's really after light?

Why doesn't glue stick to the inside of the bottle?

Why do people at baseball games sing "Take Me Out To the Ball Game" when they're already there?

Which animals in the world today have the biggest eyes?

The record is held by giant squids, which live in oceans around the world.

Their eyes are bigger than basketballs, measuring some 11-to-15 inches across.

And giant squids don't have just eight arms like the octopus. Giant squids have ten arms to go along with those big eyes.

What's been called the toughest decision any U.S. president has ever had to make?

In the summer of 1945, President Truman had to decide whether or not to drop an atom bomb on Japanese cities. He knew if he did authorize it, thousands of civilians would be killed. He knew he would go down in history as the first person (and as it turns out, the only person so far) ever to order the use of a nuclear bomb in a war.

Truman—and Truman alone—had to make the ultimate decision on whether to use nuclear bombs. He could get all the advice there was from his military and civilian advisors. But he had to make the final call. What a tough decision that was. But then, finally, one evening, sitting alone and in the dark for hours in his White House office, he made the decision.

After much soul-searching, Truman decided to do it, and many historians say it was the right decision because it hastened the end of World War II and saved the lives of many others. The European phase of the war had ended in April of 1945, but the war against Japan had raged on.

A single atom bomb was dropped on the Japanese city of Hiroshima on Aug. 6, 1945, and a second on the city of Nagasaki on Aug. 9.

That was it. Japan gave up. On the night of Aug. 14, CBS newsman Bob Trout was the first to make the official, dramatic announcement: The biggest war in history was over.

Why does the U.S. have a law saying no living person can be pictured on U.S. money?

The reason for that law goes back to one man—Salmon Chase.

He was the secretary of the treasury during the Civil War, and the word was, he was a very ambitious man who wanted to run for other political offices in the future—maybe even run for president.

While he was secretary of the treasury, Chase then put his own picture on the one-dollar bill.

Members of Congress were outraged that Chase would try for personal publicity that way—having his picture out there, increasing his visibility, to try to further his political ambitions, so Congress immediately passed a law that no living person shall be pictured on regular, circulating U.S. money. That law still exists.

In the major pro sports leagues, which teams have nicknames that have something to do with the weather?

There are five such teams:

In the National Basketball Association, there are the Miami Heat, Oklahoma City Thunder and Phoenix Suns.

In the National Hockey League, there are the Carolina Hurricanes and Tampa Bay Lightning.

There are no weather nicknames in the National Football League or major league baseball.

Which prestigious American colleges are named after a cigarette manufacturer and a beer maker?

Duke University in Durham, N.C., was originally named Trinity College. But in 1924, James Duke, the head of the American Tobacco Co., which manufactured leading cigarette brands, made a major contribution to the college, and the college changed its name from Trinity to Duke.

Vassar College in Poughkeepsie, N.Y., was created in 1861 by a large gift from Matthew Vassar. Matthew Vassar had made his money as a beer maker. He owned a prosperous brewery in Poughkeepsie.

We might point out that despite the businesses of the men their colleges were named after, underage students at Vassar are not supposed to drink beer and you'll find smoking prohibited in buildings at Duke today.

Is there an animal for each letter of the alphabet— animals whose names start with each letter of the alphabet?

Our radio listeners had fun with this game, doing it themselves and with others.

You might think Q and Z are tough, but there are well-known animals whose names start with those letters. The toughest letters to come up with are U and X, but, in any case, let's start with A, and get an animal for each letter. Here's our list. You will probably think of some other animals to include:

Alligator
Buffalo
Cat
Dog
Elephant
Frog
Giraffe
Hippopotamus
Iguana
Jaguar
Kangaroo
Leopard
Moose
Nightingale
Ostrich
Panther
Quail
Rabbit
Snake
Tiger
Unicorn (A horse-like animal with a horn on its head found in fiction and mythology)
Vulture
Whale
Xerus (An African squirrel)
Yak
Zebra

What was the eerie coincidence of the man who saved Abraham Lincoln's son?

At age 20, in 1863, Robert Lincoln, the son of Abraham Lincoln, while returning home from college, accidentally fell off a railroad platform just as a train was approaching, and was in danger of being run over by the train.

A man standing nearby saw what happened and quickly ran to the edge of the platform and reached down to pull Robert off the tracks—probably saving Robert's life. There's a question whether Robert could have climbed off the tracks in time himself, and whether the train would have been able to stop in time.

In a strange twist of fate, the man who did that—the man who pulled Robert off the tracks—the man who saved Robert Lincoln—was a famous Shakespearean actor of the day by the name of ... Edwin Booth.

Two years later, in 1865, it was Edwin Booth's brother, John Wilkes Booth, who was the man who assassinated Robert's father, Abraham Lincoln. Strange, but true.

(It is said that Edwin Booth later treasured a letter he got from Robert which thanked Edwin for saving Robert's life. That letter offered Edwin some comfort following his brother's assassination of Abraham Lincoln).

Where was the U. S. capital before it was in Washington?

Surprisingly, eight different cities served as the capital of the United States before Washington, D.C.

Philadelphia was the original capital, but then during the Revolutionary War when Philadelphia was attacked, the capital began to be constantly moved to avoid the fighting. Baltimore was the capital for a while, then Lancaster and York, Pa., Trenton and Princeton, N.J., and Annapolis, Md.

After the war, New York City was selected as the capital of the country. That's where George Washington was first inaugurated president, in 1789. But a few years later the capital was moved back to Philadelphia—and then finally, in 1800, to Washington, D.C.

What's the biggest insect in the world?

Most insects are small, but the biggest one are those called walking sticks which look like a big twig.

Walking sticks are found in many places around the world and are most prevalent in the United States in the Southeast.

Insects known as walking sticks can reach a size of over a foot in length, making them the biggest insects.

What do baseball fans have Reuben Berman to thank for?

Reuben Berman, a 31-year old stockbroker in New York, went to a big league baseball game in 1921 and a foul ball came his way while he was sitting in the stands.

Berman got the ball and kept it, but that was a no-no in those days. Fans were expected to return balls hit into the stands back to the teams. When Berman didn't, ushers and security guards descended on him.

Berman, on principal, and claiming mental and physical abuse, later filed a lawsuit. A judge ruled in Berman's favor and thereby established a fan's inalienable right to keep a baseball hit into the stands.

Fans today who keep balls hit into the stands can thank Reuben Berman.

13 a lucky number for the U.S.?

Although 13 is considered an unlucky number, the United States has done very well as a successful nation with lots of 13s, starting with winning independence with the original 13 states and having 13 stripes on the flag.

And then we come to the Great Seal of the United States which you can see on the back of the $1 dollar bill and which has an incredible number of 13s.

The eagle on the Great Seal of the U.S. holds an olive branch of 13 leaves and 13 olives in its right talon, and 13 arrows in its left.

Also on the Seal are 13 stars and 13 stripes and 13 sections of a pyramid. And inscribed on the Seal is E Pluribus Unum—which has 13 letters. The designer of the Great Seal was William Barton—13 letters in his name.

Who's the only person who was both the son AND the father of a U.S. president?

This man is unique in American history. His father was a U.S. president, and his son was a U.S. president.

He was John Harrison of North Bend, Ohio. His father was William Henry Harrison, who was elected president in 1840, and his son was Benjamin Harrison who was elected president in 1888.

What about John Harrison himself? He never made it to be president like his father and his son, but he did serve briefly in the U.S. Congress in the 1850s and spent most of his adult life tending his farm in Ohio.

What are the only 2 letters of the alphabet that don't start the name of any country in the world?

No surprise that no country's name starts with X, but what's the other letter that no country's name begins with?

The answer is W. That's kind of odd because so many other words and names start with W. But, of the 196 independent countries in the world, none starts with the letter X or W.

All the other 24 letters of the alphabet are found as the first letter of at least one country's name—even letters like Q and Z.

Q is the first letter of the Middle East country of Qatar, and Z is the first letter of the African countries of Zambia and Zimbabwe.

A question for the kids—why was the number 6 afraid?

(You have to say the answer out loud):

The number six was afraid because seven eight nine.

Which U.S. state's official symbol, on their state flag and on their state seal, shows a woman trampling a man?

A woman is shown standing on and trampling a man on the official state seal and flag of Virginia.

The woman was designed to represent virtue trampling a tyrant, signifying virtue triumphant over tyranny. George Wythe, a signer of the Declaration of Independence, designed the seal in 1776.

The official motto of Virginia is "sic semper tyrannis," or, "thus always to tyrants."

What snack food gets more free publicity than any other?

When millions of people sing "Take Me Out to the Ball Game" every year during the seventh-inning stretch at baseball games throughout the country, they sing, "Buy me some peanuts and Cracker Jack"—a free commercial for a commercial product, Cracker Jack.

And, the great thing for Cracker Jack is that baseball fans have been singing that song for over 100 years now. It was written in the early 1900s, and is still going strong.

What are some common first names of people that when not capitalized can also be everyday words?

Here are some to get you started:

There's Frank and frank, Rose and rose, Bill and bill, Mark and mark, Carol and carol, Cliff and cliff, Sue and sue.

The sixth & eighth-most populous countries in the world today didn't even exist as countries before World War II—what countries are those?

Pakistan, the sixth-most populous country in the world today was born in 1947 when the British gave India its independence and broke off two pieces of India to create the new independent countries of East Pakistan and West Pakistan on the eastern and western edges of India.

Then, it turned out the twin areas of East and West Pakistan didn't last long. By 1974, East Pakistan became a still newer country, and changed its name to Bangladesh. Then West Pakistan changed its name to just Pakistan.

Today, those relatively new countries of Pakistan and Bangladesh are two of the most populous nations on earth, with Pakistan having almost 200 million people and Bangladesh having a population of about 165 million—and to think, those countries didn't even exist before World War II.

Who was the first woman ever to run for president of the United States?

Surprisingly, it wasn't in any recent year that the first woman ran for U.S. president.

It was back in 1872 that a woman named Victoria Woodhull ran on a third-party ticket.

Woodhull, a leader in the women's suffrage movement, didn't have much of a chance because it's tough anyway for a third party candidate, and in the case of Woodhull, it was even tougher because no women could vote for her. Women still didn't have the right to vote then.

The election was won by Ulysses Grant. Victoria Woodhull got no electoral votes, but she goes down in history as the first woman ever to run for president of the United States.

What was the first family in which the mother, father and their daughter all won Oscars?

It was the family of Judy Garland.

Judy had been married to director Vincente Minnelli, and their daughter, Liza Minnelli, won the Oscar for Best Actress for "Cabaret" in 1972.

Judy's husband and Liza's father, Vincente Minnelli, won the Oscar for Best Director for "Gigi" in 1958.

And Judy Garland herself, even though she starred in lots of movies, surprisingly never won a Best Actress or even Best Supporting Actress Oscar, but she did win an honorary Oscar.

What programs labeled XXX were allowed to be shown in prime time on network TV, and parents happily and willingly let their children watch them?

This is sort of another trick question.

The Super Bowl and Olympics use Roman numerals to label their events, and the 30th Super Bowl, played in 1996, was labeled Super Bowl XXX (Super Bowl 30), and it was, of course, watched by parents and kids.

The Summer Olympics of 2012 were the 30th modern Summer Olympics and labeled Summer Olympics XXX, and also watched by families together—even though those events were XXX-labeled.

It seems easy, but many people miss this question: In counting from 1 to 100, how many 9's are there?

The answer a lot of people come up with is 19, but the correct answer is 20.

The reason many miss this question is not counting the two 9's in 99.

When did the U.S. serenade Queen Elizabeth as a tramp?

It was one of the most embarrassing things that ever happened at the White House.

When Gerald Ford was president in the 1970s, he hosted a gala state dinner honoring England's Queen Elizabeth who was visiting the United States.

During dinner, the U.S. Marine Band was playing music to serenade the guests. After dinner, President Ford asked the queen for the first dance. He led Her Majesty to the dance floor and the Marine Band played the next song on their music stands.

Of all the songs in the world, that song, as President Ford guided Queen Elizabeth to the dance floor, just happened to be ... "The Lady Is a Tramp."   Oops. That was embarrassing, but apparently the queen took it OK.

Why are lobbyists called lobbyists?

When Ulysses Grant was U.S. president from 1869 to 1877, he made a habit of relaxing most evenings at the Willard Hotel near the White House. Grant would sit in the lobby of the hotel and enjoy an after-dinner cigar.

Those seeking favors from the president found this to be an ideal opportunity. They waited for him in the lobby, and they began to be called lobbyists.

And that's how the word lobbyists came into our language to describe those seeking to influence politicians.

Why does February have only 28 days, or 29 in leap years, while all other months have 30 or 31 days?

February once did have 30 days—but it was robbed by two men.

First, Julius Caesar took a day away from February. He wanted the month named after him—July—which then had only 30 days to be longer, so he took a day from February and added it to July.

Then, after Julius Caesar, along came the Emperor Augustus. He wanted the month named for him—August—which then also had only 30 days, to have as many days as July, Julius Caesar's month. So Augustus took yet another day away from February and added it to August.

Those moves left poor February with only 28 days, or, at best, 29 in leap years.

What former all-women's college is now a power in major-college football?

For 42 years, from 1905 to 1947, Florida State University was an all-women's college.

But after World War II, many returning servicemen, using what was known as the GI Bill which provided government money to help vets pay for a college education, vastly increased college attendance. To help handle all the new students, the state of Florida opened Florida State University to men, and it became a co-ed school.

This former all-women's college then eventually became a power in major-college football, and has won several national championships.

When did the U.S. have three presidents in one year?

It's happened twice in U.S. history.

In 1841, President Martin Van Buren finished his term and was succeeded by William Henry Harrison. But Harrison died after one month in office, and Vice President John Tyler then became the third U.S. president that year.

Exactly 40 years later, in 1881, President Rutherford Hayes finished his term and was succeeded by James Garfield. But Garfield was assassinated and died after only six months in office. He was succeeded by Vice President Chester Arthur, the third president that year.

Of all the people who ever lived, which one has had the most square miles of land in the world named after him or her?

It's not even close.

By far, the most land in the world has been named after one

explorer, Amerigo Vespucci. The continents of North, Central and South America carry Amerigo Vespucci's name.

The name "America," was a modification of Amerigo Vespucci's first name and was attached to the continents by German mapmaker Martin Waldseemuller who made the first generally accepted map of the New World in 1507 and honored Vespucci who had just sailed to parts of the world that would become his namesake.

Meantime, as an addendum to this story, some historians believe Waldseemuller should not have honored Vespucci because Vespucci was only one of several explorers to the New World, and some historians feel Vespucci sailed around only part of what became known as South America, and possibly never even set foot on any of the land now named for him—but justifiably or not, North, Central and South America carry his name.

Who's the first person to have a No. 1 hit song on the Billboard charts and serve as a congressman in the U.S. Congress?

Sonny Bono had a No. 1 hit, "I Got You Babe," with his singing partner and one-time wife, Cher, in 1965. Sonny and Cher, as they were billed, were a successful singing team at that time.

Bono got into politics in the 1980s and became mayor of Palm Springs, Calif. Then in the 1990s, Bono ran for the U.S. House of Representatives from California and was elected. He served in the U.S. House from 1995 until he was killed in a skiing accident in 1998. He remains as the first member of the U.S. Congress ever to have a No. 1 hit record.

Smith is the most common last name in the U.S., but what's the most common last name in various other countries like Canada, England, France, Germany, Ireland, Italy, Mexico, Norway and Sweden?

Smith is not only the most common last name in the U.S., but it's also the most common last name in Canada and England.

In France, the most common last name is Martin. In Germany, it's Muller. In Ireland, Murphy. In Italy, Rossi or Russo. In Mexico, Martinez. In Norway, Hansen. In Sweden, Andersson.

What are the most states any candidate ever carried in a U.S. presidential election?

Two men set the record. Richard Nixon, in the 1972 election carried 49 of the 50 states when he ran against George McGovern. Nixon even carried McGovern's home state of South Dakota. The only state Nixon didn't carry was Massachusetts.

Ronald Reagan tied Nixon's record in 1984 when Reagan ran against Walter Mondale. Reagan carried 49 states, missing only Mondale's home state of Minnesota—and Reagan came close to carrying that state, too, losing Minnesota by fewer than 4,000 votes out of over two million cast. So, Reagan almost carried all 50 states.

Which 2 boys—not yet 21 years old—helped invent radio & TV?

When Philo Farnsworth was just a 16-year-old high school student in Rigby, Idaho, in 1922, he loved to experiment with electronics and in his experiments he developed what was called an image dissector. At the urging of his high school principal, Farnsworth sold his invention to RCA.

The tube that Farnsworth developed became a vital part in the creation of television, and although no one person invented TV, Farnsworth's contribution at age 16 was a major component in making TV possible.

Radio evolved from successful experiments by Guglielmo Marconi of Bologna, Italy, which began when he was a teenager.

By the time Marconi was 20 years old, in 1894, he was able to send signals over great distances through the air via wireless transmission, and that led to today's radio broadcasting.

A little 3-year-old boy caused what rule change in major league baseball?

One of the teams in the 2002 World Series was the San Francisco Giants, managed by Dusty Baker. Baker used his 3-year-old son Darren as the Giants' batboy. During one game, Darren was nearly knocked over and came close to causing interference when he wandered out on the field prematurely to retrieve a bat, and almost got in the way of a runner who was trying to cross home plate.

The next season, major league baseball instituted the "Darren Baker Rule" which sets the minimum age for batboys at 14.

What's the fastest-swimming fish?

The fish that can swim the fastest is the sailfish.

Sailfish can reach speeds of over 60 mph.

They live in warmer sections of oceans throughout the world and have a large dorsal fin that looks like a sail as they sail through the waters.

U.S. President Jimmy Carter was the first president to make what request about his name?

Carter, president from 1977 to 1981, was the first U.S. president to request that he be referred to by his nickname instead of his formal first name—in other words, that he be called Jimmy Carter instead of James Carter. Up to that time, no other president had ever done that.

Thomas Jefferson never told the press to refer to him as Tommy, James Madison never wanted to be called Jimmy, Franklin Roosevelt didn't ask to be called Frankie.

Some presidents like Abraham Lincoln and Theodore Roosevelt have sometimes been referred to with a nickname, like Abe or Teddy respectively—but not because of their request. Carter was the first president to specifically ask to be known by his nickname.

When in major league baseball was "Who" really on first?

There was the famous Abbott & Costello comedy routine of "Who's on First." The funny thing is, years after Abbott & Costello introduced that routine, it actually happened for real in major league baseball games.

A player from Taiwan joined the Los Angeles Dodgers in 2007 and got a base hit. His name: Hu Chin-Lung. In his language, "Hu" is pronounced "Who," so when Hu Chin-Lung was standing at first base after his hit, you could say, in truth, "Who's on first."

Hu Chin-Lung has had a short major league career. He played briefly with the Dodgers in 2007 and 2008 and with the New York Mets in 2011, and then returned to play in Asian baseball leagues, but he goes down in history as a man who truly was "Who's on First."

And we did a little research, and found that there was a second baseman in the majors briefly in 1920 whose name was Allie Watt—so for him, you could have said, in reality, "What's on Second," just like in the Abbott & Costello routine.

Surprise—what's the biggest city in the U.S.?

If you told someone that the biggest city in the U.S. was NOT New York City, Los Angeles or Chicago, but Sitka, Alaska, they'd probably think you were wrong. But, we're talking here about area, not population—and the biggest city in the U.S. in area is not any of the big population cities like New York City or Los Angeles or Chicago. It is Sitka, Alaska.

Sitka has 4,811 square miles in its official city limits. By contrast, New York City has 468, Los Angeles 503 and Chicago 234.

In the lower 48 states, the city with the largest area is Jacksonville, Fla., whose city limits are composed of 885 square miles.

Who are some famous people whose last names are the same as words used in religions?

There's former Senator Frank Church

English poet Alexander Pope

Actress Eva Marie Saint

Comedian Joey Bishop

Movie star Shirley Temple

Band leader Tony Pastor

Entertainer Eddie Cantor

U.S. Treasurer Ivy Baker Priest

What dead man was elected to the U.S. Senate?

Mel Carnahan of Missouri ran for the U.S. Senate in 2000, but was killed in a plane crash during the campaign. The plane he was riding on, incidentally, was piloted by his son Randy who was also killed.

Because the election law in Missouri would not allow for Carnahan's name to be taken off the ballot at that late date, Carnahan was listed on Election Day as the Democratic nominee, facing Republican John Ashcroft.

Despite being deceased, Carnahan won the election. The Missouri governor then appointed Carnahan's widow, Jean, to fill his seat in the Senate until a special election to be held two years later. She served in the Senate until defeated in that 2002 election.

Ashcroft, who lost to a dead man, was appointed attorney general in the cabinet of President George W. Bush, and served from 2001 to 2005.

Why were sandwiches named after the Earl of Sandwich?

John Montagu, whose title was the fourth Earl of Sandwich, was a British nobleman who served in several capacities in the British government in the 1700s, including being the first lord of the admiralty.

Lord Sandwich is credited with popularizing the idea of sandwiches. He loved to gamble and hated to leave the gambling table. He would have his servant put a slice of meat between two pieces of bread so he could hold his food in one hand and eat, while continuing to stay in the game, making his gambling moves with his other hand.

Soon, that way of serving food was named after him.

Which animal has appeared most often in movie history?

It's a lion, seen before MGM movies since the 1920s.

Why did MGM pick a lion for its logo?

When the company was founded in 1924, they asked their publicity man, Howard Dietz, to come up with a logo. Dietz had gone to Columbia University whose nickname is the Lions—so Dietz chose a lion to identify MGM movies.

What was so strange about 2 foul balls hit by Richie Ashburn?

Richie Ashburn had a long career in major league baseball, playing in the majors from 1948 to 1962—and he had one odds-defying at bat in 1957.

In a game that year, Ashburn hit a foul ball into the stands that unfortunately hit a woman in her face, and as it turned out, broke her nose—but that's not the end of the story.

Ushers quickly ran to the woman after she had been hit, and lifted her out of her seat and began taking her to the first-aid room a few sections away. Meantime, Ashburn had stepped out of the batter's box and watched for a moment as she was being attended to. Ashburn tipped his cap to her, signifying he was so sorry his foul ball had hit her, and to show that he wished her good luck.

Then, Ashburn stepped back into the batter's box to await the next pitch. The pitch came in, and Ashburn fouled it off again. In a million-to-one shot, that foul ball hit the same woman in a different part of the ballpark as she was being taken through the stands to the first-aid room. That foul ball broke her knee.

What are the odds that with thousands of people in the ballpark, a batter would hit two foul balls on two consecutive pitches that would both hit the same person who was in two different locations in the stands.

How's it possible that Stanley Dunham gave birth to a future U.S. president?

Stanley Dunham did give birth to a president, President Barack Obama.

Stanley Dunham was a female. When she was born, she was given the first name of Stanley by her father, Stanley Dunham Sr. He wanted a child named after him, and when he got a girl instead of a boy, he still named the baby Stanley.

Her full birth name was Stanley Ann Dunham. As a child, she went by Stanley and was often teased by many other kids. When she reached adulthood, she began using her middle name and went by Ann.

She gave birth to Barack Obama in 1961. Stanley Ann Dunham died of cancer in 1995 at age 53.

Who or what is Roy G. Biv?

The colors of a rainbow are always in the same order—red, orange, yellow, green, blue, indigo and violet, and an easy way to remember the colors, and their order, is the name Roy G. Biv.

Take the letters of Roy G. Biv to remember the order of colors— red, orange, yellow, green, blue, indigo and violet.

Why is Alzheimer's disease called Alzheimer's?

Alzheimer's disease is named after Dr. Alois Alzheimer.

He was a German physician who is acknowledged for his research and the first published data on what became known as Alzheimer's disease.

Dr. Alzheimer did his work on identifying the disease in the early 1900s. He had a relatively short life himself. He died of heart failure in 1915 at the age of 51.

Which major U.S. airport is named after a man who shot down airplanes?

Chicago's O'Hare airport is named after Edward (Butch) O'Hare who became a hero because he shot down airplanes.

O'Hare was a U.S. Navy pilot in World War II. He single-handedly shot down five enemy aircraft over the Pacific in a famous air battle, and was awarded the Medal of Honor.

After the war, Chicago honored hometown hero O'Hare by naming what had been previously called Orchard Airport after Butch O'Hare, and it became O'Hare Airport.

By the way, if you've ever wondered why the code for O'Hare Airport is ORD, that comes from the first two letters and the last letter of the airport's original name of Orchard.

When did the U.S. have to wait 4 months after a presidential election to find out who won?

That's how long it took—four months after the 1876 election—to figure out which presidential candidate, Rutherford Hayes or Sam Tilden, was the winner.

The delay was caused by a dispute over the electoral votes in four states. The dispute dragged on and on while the country waited and waited to find out who their new president would be.

The question about the electoral votes was thrown into Congress where it was hotly debated day after day. Finally, a 15-man committee was chosen to select the winner. After a close 8-7 vote, Hayes, on March 2, 1877, was declared the victor—about four months after the November Election Day.

Who invented the flush toilet?   (His name lives on)

Although several inventors have claimed to be the inventor of the modern flush toilet, many historians say Thomas Crapper of England deserves the most credit. For one thing, he installed the first flush toilet for Queen Victoria in 1884—and his name lives on as a slang term for a toilet itself, and the first four letters of his name live on as well.

Another man who worked on early flush toilets was England's Sir John Harrington whose first name, John, became a euphemism for bathrooms—as in, "I'm going to the john."

What's strange about Easter Island?

One of the most intriguing places in the world is a far-off island in the South Pacific, 2,400 miles west of Chile.

On this remote island, called Easter Island because it was discovered on an Easter Sunday years ago, there are more than 800 strange statues, 30 to 40 feet tall, and weighing 60 to 70 tons.

They're strange because they have out-of-this-world faces. Strange because they were able to be moved long ago from the mountain rock from which they were carved out to open fields where they are today.

How were those enormous statues moved, and why do those faces look like possible aliens? No one now knows, but some have even suggested that aliens from outer space visited here and left them behind as a sort of calling card.

Those statues on Easter Island remain an intriguing, unsolved mystery.

Which are the only U.S. states that have all three letters "u," "s," and "a" in their names?

There are just four such states:

They are Louisiana, Massachusetts, South Carolina and South Dakota.

How did Coca-Cola get that name?

When drug store owner John Pemberton invented a new soft drink in 1886 in Atlanta, he didn't know what to call it. He discussed his dilemma with his bookkeeper, Frank Robinson.

Robinson, who had no experience in advertising or marketing, then single-handedly came up with what many experts say is now the most recognized brand name in the world.

Robinson looked at two of the ingredients in Pemberton's beverage and suggested "coca" from the flavoring of coca leaves and "kola" from the flavoring of kola nuts—but to make both words start with the same letter, Robinson changed kola to cola, thereby creating the name Coca-Cola.

An added part to this story is that Robinson wrote out the words Coca-Cola in his own distinctive flowing handwriting, and the way he wrote it is still used by Coca-Cola today as its world-famous distinctive trademark—all from a guy who was not in the advertising or marketing business and not in the business of naming new products.

Maybe there's a lesson there.

Who's been the smartest U.S. president?

You can get lots of discussion and arguments about who's been the smartest president—but here's a story about a dinner President John Kennedy once held, and his choice for the smartest president.

Kennedy hosted a White House dinner one evening for a group of Nobel Prize winners, and before dinner he stood up and gave this toast to the group:

He said there was more brain power in the White House dining room that night than at any other time in White House history—with the possible exception of when Thomas Jefferson dined alone.

That's a pretty good vote for Jefferson.

Actually, Jefferson was a man of many talents. His talents covered an amazing range.

He wrote the Declaration of Independence.

He became a leading architect of his time, designing the Virginia Capitol building, along with buildings at the University of Virginia and his own famous home, Monticello.

He was a scientific farmer, creating new farming techniques to help farmers, and he cultivated some of the finest gardens in America.

His many inventions included the swivel chair and the dumb-waiter.

His excellent personal book collection became the nucleus of the Library of Congress.

He wrote Virginia's civil code and founded the University of Virginia.

He devised the convenient decimal system of coinage allowing

Americans to use dollars and cents instead of England's shillings and pounds.

He learned Latin, Greek and French, studied law and was admitted to the bar. He prepared written vocabularies of American Indian languages.

He was an accomplished musician, playing the violin in chamber music concerts.

He served as a successful U.S. diplomat. He made the Louisiana Purchase which doubled the size of the United States. And, he gets high marks from most historians for his two terms as U.S. president.

Tom was pretty smart.

There are just 8 countries in the world whose names end in the letter "y"—and they are all well-known countries. Which countries are those?

Those eight countries are, in alphabetical order, Germany, Hungary, Italy, Norway, Paraguay, Turkey, Uruguay and Vatican City.

How was it possible for a man to go to bed at 11 p.m. on Sept. 2, sleep 8 hours, and when he woke up, it was already Sept. 14?

This actually happened in America.

Eleven days were completely eliminated in September 1752 when the calendar was changed from the old Roman calendar to the

Gregorian calendar we use today.

When the change was made, 11 days were dropped to line up with the new calendar. The country went directly from Sept. 2 right to Sept. 14.

The days from Sept. 3 through Sept. 13 never existed that year. We wonder if people complained then that their lives had just been shortened by 11 days.

What did the football coach at Youngstown State College invent that's now seen at all football games?

Before 1941, when officials during a football game saw a penalty they blew a horn or a whistle. That was often confused with the whistle that ended a play, and players would stop prematurely. Also fans and media often didn't know a penalty had been called because they might not have heard the horn or whistle. To remedy the problem, Dike Beede, the football coach at Youngstown State College in Ohio, invented…the penalty flag.

Beede got the idea of having officials throw a flag when they saw a penalty. His wife Irma made the first ones and they were used at a game between Youngstown and Oklahoma City University on Oct. 17, 1941, in Youngstown, Ohio.

So the next time you see a football game and see an official throw a penalty flag, know that it was Dike Beede who started it all. His wife has been called the "Betsy Ross of Football" since she made the first penalty flags. She had used an old bed sheet and curtain weights. Today's penalty flags are a yellow cloth filled with sand at one end to keep them from blowing around.

Of all the cities in the U.S. that have a population of 40,000 or more and have just a one-word name, which city has the longest name?

It's Charlottesville, Va., whose name has 15 letters in it.

Charlottesville is the home of the University of Virginia and was the home of Presidents Thomas Jefferson and James Monroe.

The city was named after Queen Charlotte of England, the wife of King George III.

Today, no other one-word U.S. city over 40,000 population can match Charlottesville in the length of its name.

Which U.S. president spent some time in prison?

The president who spent some time in prison was Andrew Jackson.

As a youth, Jackson had fought in the Revolutionary War, and during the war, he was captured by the British and spent time as a prisoner of war at a prison in Camden, S.C.

Later in his life, Jackson would go on to a high-ranking military career. He became a war hero in the War of 1812, and became U.S. president in 1829.

What daily radio show was so popular that movie theaters used to stop their movies so the audience could hear the radio show?

It's hard to realize now how popular the "Amos 'n' Andy" radio show was in the 1930s.

It was broadcast 15 minutes a night, Mondays through Fridays, and had an incredible audience. Many theater owners across America, afraid that people would stay home to listen to "Amos 'n' Andy" and not come to a movie, let it be known that they would stop the movie when "Amos 'n' Andy" came on, and pipe the radio show into the theater so the movie audience wouldn't miss the latest episode of "Amos 'n' Andy." The movie would resume after "Amos 'n' Andy" signed off for the night.

There's never been another radio series like that.

In its radio heyday in the 1930s, Amos and Andy were played by Freeman Godsen and Charles Correll. Godsen and Correll also did the voices of other people in the cast. And, Godsen and Correll, along with their announcer, Bill Hay, wrote each night's show.

Eventually the show went to 30 minutes once a week, and then moved to TV, without Godsen and Correll, but it then never achieved the amazing popularity it once had.

Which U.S. cities have the same name as a sport?

There's La Crosse, Wisc.

And, how about Bowling Green, Ky.,
and Bowling Green, Ohio.

You might also want to include Olympia, Wash., which has the
same name as the site of the first Olympic Games in Greece.

The presidential retreat, Camp David, was named after a 6-year-old boy. Who was that boy?

Camp David, was originally built for President Franklin Roosevelt
in the 1940s, and Roosevelt called it Shangri-La after the fictional
Himalayan paradise.

But when Dwight Eisenhower became president in the 1950s, he
changed the name from Shangri-La to Camp David—naming it
after his 6-year-old grandson, David Eisenhower, and Camp David
has remained its name ever since.

Incidentally, that 6-year-old grandson, David Eisenhower, grew up
to marry Julie Nixon, the daughter of President Richard Nixon—
and that's the only case in history in which the grandson of one
U.S. president married the daughter of another U.S. president.

How far can you see on a clear day with the naked eye?

When you ask the average person how far they can see with the naked eye on a clear day, you might get answers that range from a mile to several miles, depending on where they are, but many people don't think about looking up in the sky.

You can see 93 million miles with the naked eye when you look at the sun because that's how far away it is.

And, that's far from the limit of the average naked eye. At night you can see stars that are billions of miles away.

Who was U.S. president for one day?

In 1849, President James Polk's four-year term ended and the new president, Zachary Taylor, was to be inaugurated.

But Inauguration Day fell on a Sunday that year and Taylor refused to take the oath on a Sunday because of his religious beliefs. Polk's term ended at noon—so the U.S. was without a president from noon Sunday until noon Monday when Taylor would be sworn in.

Next in line under the Constitution rules in those days was the president pro tem of the Senate, David Atchison. Technically Atchison was president for those 24 hours.

What did he do on that one day he was president? Atchison later said he spent much of the day sleeping.

On his gravestone in his home state of Missouri, it says, "Here lies David Atchison, President of the United States For One Day."

William Dawes was an American hero, but he is forgotten today because of his name—what was wrong with his name?

When Paul Revere made his historic ride on the eve of the American Revolution to warn colonists that the British army was coming, another man rode with Revere and did just as much as Revere and was just as heroic. He was William Dawes, but today Revere is remembered and Dawes is not.

It's all because of the rhyming of Dawes' and Revere's names.

Revere is remembered because of Henry Wadsworth Longfellow's famous poem, "Listen my children and you shall hear, of the midnight ride of Paul Revere." Dawes is a forgotten man because his name didn't rhyme like Revere's when Longfellow sat down to write that immortal line, "Listen my children and you shall hear..."

Which is more: $1,000 a day for 30 days, or one penny doubled each day for a month?

If someone offered you a job for $1,000 a day for 30 days—that's $30,000—or one penny doubled each day for 30 days, which would you take?

If you took one penny doubled each day for a month, you'd wind up with over $5 million.

That seems impossible because the second day you'd get just two pennies, the third day just four pennies, and so on—but mathematical progression takes over.

By the tenth day you get $5.12. Keep doubling that and by the fifteenth day you'd be up to $163.84. By the twentieth day, $5,242.88. By the twenty-fifth day, $167,772.16. And by the thirtieth day, $5,368,709.12.

What was highly unusual about the baseball trade involving pitchers Mike Kekich and Fritz Peterson?

This wasn't your everyday baseball trade.

Mike Kekich and Fritz Peterson were both pitchers for the New York Yankees in 1973. Then came the trade.

Kekich and Peterson traded wives. Mrs. Kekich became Mrs. Peterson, and Mrs. Peterson went with Kekich.

Soon after that trade, the Yankees sent Kekich to the Cleveland Indians.

What is the most abundant animal in the world?

There are more ants in the world than any other animal—and there's a bit of an oddity about that.

Ants are found on every continent in the world—except the one continent whose name starts with "Ant." That, of course, is Antarctica, the one place where there are no ants.

Two places were named after U.S. presidents—but then their names were unceremoniously taken away. Who were those presidents, and where are those places?

After President John Kennedy was assassinated in 1963, his successor, President Lyndon Johnson, wanted to honor Kennedy, and Johnson signed an executive order changing the name of Cape Canaveral, Fla., to Cape Kennedy, Fla. Johnson picked that particular location to honor Kennedy because of Kennedy's support of the space program and his challenge to the U.S. to send humans to the moon in that decade.

Cape Canaveral remained Cape Kennedy for 10 years—but in 1973, residents in the area voted to go back to the original name. Kennedy's name was taken away, and the town of Cape Kennedy became Cape Canaveral again, which it is today.

Something similar happened involving another president. When a town was settled in New Hampshire in 1800, John Adams was president, and the town was named Adams, N.H. But 28 years later when Adams' son, President John Quincy Adams, ran for another term and was defeated by Andrew Jackson, the folks in Adams, N.H., took the name Adams away and changed the name of their town from Adams, N.H. to Jackson, N.H. It's still Jackson, N.H. today. The name "Adams" is no longer honored there.

What was ironic about all these famous movies— "My Fair Lady," "The Music Man," "Easter Parade," "Long Day's Journey Into Night," and "Titanic"?

All these award-winning movies, which are all so different from each other in content, were, ironically, all set in the exact same year, 1912. The action in each of these films takes place in 1912.

The movies themselves were released in different years— "My Fair Lady" came out in 1964, "The Music Man" in 1962, "Easter Parade" in 1948, "Long Day's Journey Into Night" in 1962, and "Titanic" in 1997—but their stories all occur in 1912.

Why do they use the word love in tennis instead of zero?

The score of love in tennis came from the French word "l'oeuf," which means egg. An egg looks something like a zero.

In the early days of tennis, when the game was more genteel, it was thought bad form to tell an opponent he or she had a score of zero or nothing, so "love" was adopted from the French word for egg to make it sound better, and that word "love" for zero has lasted all these years in tennis.

Why do we put points on stars?

When you see a star that is drawn or printed, like, for instance, the stars on a flag, the stars have points. You see five-point stars, six-point stars, etc.—but the fact is, real stars in the sky have no points. They are round. The sun is a star. It's round, like other real stars.

Nobody seems to know why humans put points on stars when they draw or print them.

Almost all colleges in America have the name of a city, state or person in the name of the college—but which few colleges don't have a city, state or person's name in their name?

There aren't many, but here are a few:

There are the service academies, Army, Navy and Air Force plus Northwestern and Southern Methodist University (SMU).

Can you think of any more?

What's the difference between England, Britain, Great Britain, the United Kingdom and the U.K.?

If you're in London, England, you're in a country that has more names than any other nation. You could say you're in England or Britain or Great Britain or the United Kingdom or the U.K. Whew.

But there is a difference.

The names Britain or Great Britain refer to a combination of England plus Scotland and Wales. The names United Kingdom or U.K., consist of Great Britain—that's England, Scotland and Wales—plus Northern Ireland.

The funny thing is, if you buy one of their stamps, you won't find any name. England was the first country in the world to issue postage stamps and they have permission of the International Postal Union to be the only nation that doesn't use their name on stamps. Maybe they don't know what name to use.

What year came after 1 B.C.?

You could say that one year was skipped in human history.

After the year 1 B.C., calendar measurement immediately went to A.D. 1. There was no year numbered zero between 1 B.C. and A.D. 1, although in centuries since, there have been zero years such as 100, 1900, 2000, etc.

When did Mother's Day start—and who started it?

Mother's Day was conceived by a school teacher in Grafton, W.Va., Anna Jarvis.

Her mother died on May 9, 1905, and after that, Anna honored her mother by holding memorial services for her mom each year on the second Sunday in May.

That gave Anna the idea of honoring all mothers and she began writing hundreds of letters, campaigning for an annual observance of Mother's Day.

By 1914, through Anna's efforts, President Woodrow Wilson proclaimed Mother's Day nationally—always to be on the second Sunday in May.

One other fact about Anna Jarvis: Anna, the founder and promoter of Mother's Day, was never a mother herself.

And how about Father's Day?

The idea for Father's Day came to a woman in church one day in 1910 in Spokane, Wash.

Sonora Dodd thought about her father—how he had sacrificed to raise her and her brothers after her mother had died.

She proposed a Father's Day celebration to her minister. He agreed and got other Spokane clergymen to go along. The first Father's Day service was held in Spokane a few weeks later. Newspapers carried the story of that Father's Day observance and the idea spread.

That first Father's Day was held on the third Sunday of June. The next year it was held on that day again, and that began the tradition of Father's Day always being on the third Sunday in June.

Shortly after World War II, why was there no U.S. president in the White House for almost 4 years?

In 1948, the White House was almost 150 years old and badly in need of structural repairs and renovations.

Rather than have the president live and work there during all the mess while extensive repairs and reconstruction were being made, it was decided to move the president, his family and staff, across the street to Blair House.

Blair House is a four-story mansion usually used as a guesthouse for top-ranking foreign visitors, but for almost four years, it served as the home and office for the U.S. president at the time, Harry Truman. Truman, his family and staff moved out of the White House in late 1948 and didn't return until March of 1952.

During all that time, there was no president in the White House.

How far did the Dow Jones industrial average fall during the Great Depression?

Between September 1929 and July 1932, the Dow fell an incredible 89 percent.

It reached its low on July 8, 1932 when it closed that day at 41.22.

That wasn't the only grim figure of the Great Depression. More than 10,000 banks in the United States failed. Factories shut down. Stores closed. The unemployment rate in the 1930s eventually grew to a staggering 23.6 percent.

The theme song of the Great Depression was a popular song of the day, "Brother, Can You Spare A Dime?"

How long did it take the Dow to climb to just 500 after its plunge in the Great Depression?

It took an unbelievably long time for the Dow to reach even 500 after the Depression.

From its low of 41 in 1932, it took more than 20 years for the Dow to climb to just 500, which it finally did in 1956.

Surprisingly, the Dow never got above 1,000 until 1972.

Which U.S. president used to regularly swim—nude— in the Potomac River, while he was president?

John Quincy Adams, president from 1825 to 1829, left the White House many afternoons to take a nude dip in the Potomac.

All went well until one day when a woman reporter, who had been trying unsuccessfully to get an interview with Adams, went to the banks of the Potomac, grabbed Adams' clothes and threatened to keep them unless he agreed to give her the interview. We have to remember there was no Secret Service to guard presidents in those days, and Adams often went alone for his nude swim.

Adams had no choice after the woman's ultimatum. He got out of the water, put his clothes on while she discretely turned away, and the reporter got her exclusive interview.

Which actor changed the way Oscar winners are announced?

Before 1970, when an Oscar winner was announced, the presenter would open the envelope and say, "And, the winner is…" But then when George C. Scott won the Best Actor Oscar for his performance in the movie "Patton" in 1970, he refused to accept the Oscar, saying the use of the word "winner" implied there were losers, and there should not be winners and losers among actors.

The Academy took his advice. Starting the next year, the Academy told presenters to say, "And the Oscar goes to…" instead of saying, "And the winner is…" And they've been following that ever since.

What are the longest words that have all their letters in alphabetical order, and what are the longest words with all letters in reverse alphabetical order?

For a fun word game, see how many words you can think of in which all the letters in the word are in alphabetical order, and conversely, see how many words you can think of in which all the letters in the word are in reverse alphabetical order—and the longer the word the better. Here are some examples:

Words with all letters in alphabetical order can include these six-letter words: almost, begins, biopsy. There's also a seven-letter word: billowy

Words with all letters in reverse alphabetical order include these five-letter words: spoke, polka, and two seven-letter words: wronged, sponged.

In which sport does the ball travel the fastest?

It's the sport of jai alai, where players fling the ball out of basket-type gloves they wear, called cestas.

Jai alai players can fling that ball out of their cestas at speeds close to 200 mph.

How hot can it get—what's the hottest outdoor temperature ever recorded in the U.S., and where did that happen?

The all-time weather bureau record for the hottest day ever in the U.S. is 134 degrees Fahrenheit. That record was set on July 10, 1913 at Death Valley, Calif.

Interestingly, that is also now considered the world record, too. Previously the record for the hottest day ever officially recorded anywhere on Earth was 136 degrees Fahrenheit, in Libya, Africa, in 1922. But recent research has questioned the instruments and methods used in determining that temperature.

So, Death Valley, Calif., is now both the U.S., and the world leader in having the hottest day.

What county sheriff became president of the United States?

Grover Cleveland was a sheriff in Erie County, N.Y., from 1871 to 1873, and then had an unusually quick rise from that job to the presidency.

After serving as sheriff, he was elected mayor of Buffalo, then governor of New York, and, in 1884, president of the United States.

Amazingly, Cleveland went from sheriff to president in just 11 years.

What's the only U.S. state with just a one-syllable name?

Of all the 50 U.S. states, the only one that has just a one syllable name is the state of Maine.

It's well known that Irving Berlin wrote "God Bless America," but who wrote that other great patriotic song, "America the Beautiful"?

Actually two people wrote "America the Beautiful"—and the odd thing is, they never knew each other.

A teacher from Wellesley College, 33-year-old Katherine Lee Bates, wrote the words to "America the Beautiful," in 1893.

Her words were eventually matched to the music of an old hymn, "Materna," written years before by a New Jersey church organist, Samuel Ward.

Bates never met Ward. He had died before knowing his "Materna" hymn would become the music for one of America's favorite patriotic songs.

Bates did live to enjoy its popularity—she died in 1929—but she could never share its success with her co-writer.

It was a coincidence that Bates wrote "America the Beautiful" in the first place. She was on vacation in the summer of 1893 and visited friends in Colorado. One day they happened to take her up to Pike's Peak. Bates was so enthralled with the view from there that she immediately wrote down the first draft of the words to "America the Beautiful." ("O beautiful for spacious skies, for amber waves of grain. For purple mountain majesties above the fruited plain")

But just think: If she had not vacationed in Colorado, and if her friends had not happened to take her up to Pike's Peak, the nation might not have the song "America the Beautiful."

There are 8 independent countries in the world and just 2 U.S. states whose names end in "land"—which countries and states are they?

The countries that end in "land" are England, Finland, Iceland, Ireland, New Zealand, Poland, Swaziland and Switzerland.

The two U.S. states that end in "land" are Maryland and Rhode Island.

Is there a spider hidden on $1 bills?

Some claim there's not only a picture of a spider on $1 bills, but also an owl—but to see them you have to have good eyes, perhaps a magnifying glass, and some might say a good imagination.

If you look closely in the upper right corner on the front of the $1 bill, there's a shield with the number 1. In the upper left curve of the shield, there's a little figure that some say is a spider.
As for the owl, look at the tallest leaf to the left of the spider, and there's a figure that some say is an owl.

The U.S. Treasury Department claims no knowledge as to whether the artist did or did not put a spider and owl on the $1 bill when the present bill was designed in 1929, but supporters of the spider-and-owl theory say they were placed there as good luck symbols. One jokester has said though that if $1 bills were lucky, they'd be $100 bills.

Who was the first U.S. president born west of the Mississippi? (It took a long time till that happened)

From the time the first U.S. president, George Washington, took office in 1789, through the next—would you believe—140 years, every president was born east of the Mississippi.

The first president born west of the Mississippi was the president who took office in 1929, Herbert Hoover. Hoover had been born in West Branch, Iowa.

What countries have changed their name?

It's amazing how many countries in the world have changed their name.

For instance, Indonesia used to be the Dutch East Indies.
Belize used to be British Honduras.
Bangladesh used to be East Pakistan.
Thailand used to be Siam.
Iran used to be Persia.
Zambia used to be Northern Rhodesia.
Zimbabwe used to be Southern Rhodesia.
The Democratic Republic of the Congo used to be Zaire.
Ghana used to be the Gold Coast.
Myanmar used to be Burma.
Sri Lanka used to be Ceylon.
Ethiopia used to be Abyssinia
Jordan used to be Transjordan
And, Russia used to be called the Soviet Union. It's interesting to note that no major nation ever had its name wiped off the map in so short of time as the Soviet Union. While it existed, the Soviet Union was the biggest country in the world in size, and one of the most powerful and feared, yet that name "Soviet Union" for Russia and its republics lasted only 69 years from its creation in 1922 until it was disbanded in 1991.

In what clever way did a man beat a death sentence?

There's an old legend that in a far-off land many years ago, a king sentenced a man to die. And then the king gave the man a choice on how he wanted to die.

The man thought for a moment and then announced the way he chose to die. He said, "I choose old age."

He's not well known, but what 2 uncanny books did Morgan Robertson write?

Morgan Robertson, in 1898—14 years before the Titanic sank—wrote a book about a ship he named the Titan. In his fiction book, the Titan was the biggest ship in the world. It was described as unsinkable. It was on its maiden voyage from England to the U.S. In mid-April, it hit an iceberg in the North Atlantic and sank. There were not enough lifeboats and many people perished. Just about EVERYTHING Robertson wrote about in his 1898 fiction book actually came true when the real, similarly named, Titanic sailed and sank 14 years later, in 1912.

But that's not all about this man, Robertson.

In the early 1900s, he wrote a short story, titled "Beyond the Spectrum." This eerie story that Robertson wrote accurately described events in World War II—a war that was still many years away. Robertson even had America's entry into the war coming from a surprise attack by Japan. He wrote that 27 years before it happened.

What unusual thing did the Chicago White Sox wear in a big league baseball game in 1976?

Bill Veeck, former flamboyant owner of the White Sox, thought he had a great idea for both hot-weather play and publicity.

He had his team wear shorts instead of regular baseball pants for Chicago's doubleheader against Kansas City on August 8, 1976.

It didn't work. The idea was booed by fans at the game and ridiculed by the other team. It also made sliding tough on Chicago's players.

Wearing shorts in big league baseball had a short life. The White Sox went back to their regular uniforms for the second game that day, and never wore the shorts again.

We know Juneau, Alaska, is the northern-most capital city in the U.S., and Honolulu is the southern-most, but excluding Alaska and Hawaii, what are the northern-most, southern-most, eastern-most and western-most capital cities of U.S. states?

In the 48 contiguous states, the northern-most capital city is Olympia, Washington.

The southern-most is Austin, Texas.

The eastern-most is Augusta, Maine.

And, the western-most is Salem, Oregon.

How's it possible that a man got the most popular votes in a presidential election AND the most Electoral College votes, yet still lost the election— how is that possible?

It was one of the strangest presidential elections in U.S. history:

Andrew Jackson ran against John Quincy Adams in 1824. Although Jackson had the most popular votes and the most Electoral College votes (which are the ones that count), he didn't have a majority of the Electoral College votes. The Constitution says a winner must have not only the most Electoral College votes, but also a majority of Electoral College votes.

The election was complicated by the fact that two others also ran and got some Electoral College votes. The final Electoral College vote total was 99 for Jackson, 84 for Adams, 41 for William Crawford and 37 for Henry Clay. There were 261 Electoral College votes then, and to be a winner and have a majority, a candidate needed 131 Electoral College votes, so Jackson's 99 were not enough.

Under the Constitution, if nobody gets a majority of Electoral College votes, the election is thrown into the House of Representatives. In this election, even though Jackson had the most popular AND Electoral College votes, the House chose Adams to be president when Crawford and Clay's backers in the House eventually gave their support to Adams.

Jackson did get revenge four years later. He ran against Adams again and this time beat him decisively without the election having to be thrown into the House of Representatives.

Do U.S. Supreme Court justices have to be law school graduates?

Surprisingly, U.S. Supreme Court justices are not required to have any legal training—or even to have gone to law school.

That's hard to believe because those judges rule on some of the most complex legal questions in the nation.

But nowhere in the Constitution does it say that Supreme Court justices have to be lawyers or have any legal training. In fact, several justices in the court's history had never attended law school, and one justice, James Byrnes, for instance, who served on the court in the 1940s, had never attended high school, college or law school.

Why is the Kentucky Derby called a Derby?

The Kentucky Derby got its unusual name from a British earl.

In 1780, a British sportsman, the Earl of Derby, founded a popular horse race in Epsom, England. The annual race was named in his honor, and called Derby's race at Epsom, or the Epsom Derby.

When the folks in Kentucky inaugurated their annual race in 1875, they wanted it to sound big-time so they borrowed the name of the big race in Britain—the Epsom Derby—and called their race the Kentucky Derby. And that's why the Kentucky Derby is called a Derby.

Do we really have the right date for the July 4 holiday?

Contrary to popular opinion, the Declaration of Independence was not signed by the majority of the members of Congress on July 4, 1776.

Most members of Congress didn't sign the Declaration until August 2, so some historians feel August 2 should be Independence Day.

But wait.

Others think it should be July 2 because that was the day Congress approved by voice vote the resolution of having a Declaration of Independence. Strictly speaking, that became the official date of declaring independence by the United States. Then it was July 4 that Congress, in another vote, approved the final draft of the Declaration, but most members didn't sign it until August 2.

So, is Independence Day really July 2, July 4, or August 2? Logically, any of those days could be Independence Day, but July 4 it is.

Who's been the only U.S. president who's had the biggest city in 2 different states named after him?

That honor goes to Andrew Jackson.

The biggest city in population in Florida is Jacksonville, and the biggest city in population in Mississippi is Jackson.

Both were named after Andrew Jackson.

Why is it called the Dow Jones average?

The Dow Jones industrial average and the Dow Jones company almost had a different name.

The Dow Jones company was founded in 1882 by a New York newspaper business reporter, Charles Dow. He took in two partners to help form his company, Edward Jones and Charles Bergstresser.

They could have called it the Dow Jones Bergstesser company, but they made the decision to call it just the Dow Jones company. They left Mr. Bergstresser's name off, and nobody is sure today how he felt about that, but they sure saved everybody over the years a lot of time on the air and space in newspapers by not calling it the Dow Jones Bergstresser company and the Dow Jones Bergstresser average.

But poor Mr. Bergstresser. His name is forgotten.

Who's the only person who ever hit a home run in major league baseball AND scored a touchdown in the NFL—in the same week?

This remarkable feat was accomplished by Deion Sanders.

He was playing major league baseball for the New York Yankees in 1989, and on Sept. 5 hit a homer for the Yanks. Then he left the Yankees to fulfill his contract to play football with the Atlanta Falcons of the NFL, and that same week he, amazingly, scored a touchdown in the NFL for the Falcons.

Sanders had a relatively long career with several different teams in both sports. He played in the NFL from 1989 to 2005, and in major league baseball from 1989 to 2001.

He's also the only person to play in both a World Series and a Super Bowl. Sanders played in the World Series with the Atlanta Braves in 1992, and he played in the Super Bowl with two teams, the San Francisco 49ers in 1995 and the Dallas Cowboys in 1996.

What does the name melba toast have to do with an opera singer?

Opera star Nellie Melba was appearing in London in the 1890s and told the chef at the Savoy Hotel where she was staying that she was trying to lose some weight. She asked the chef to cut her slices of toast as thin as possible. The chef, the famous Auguste Escoffier, came up with a new creation of thin, crisp slices that he named in honor of Nellie Melba, calling it melba toast—a name that lives on.

At the end of her stay in London, a party was given for Ms. Melba, and Escoffier created a special dessert that he named for her—a dessert of ice cream, peaches, and rich sauces that he called peach melba, another name that lives on.

(We wonder if some of the weight Ms. Melba lost while eating melba toast might have been gained back when she had the peach melba dessert).

What is it about men named Francis and U.S. patriotism?

By coincidence, the men who wrote "The Star-Spangled Banner," "My Country 'tis of Thee," and the Pledge of Allegiance to the Flag, all had first or middle names of Francis.

Francis Scott Key wrote "The Star-Spangled Banner," Samuel Francis Smith wrote "My Country 'tis of Thee," and Francis Bellamy wrote the Pledge of Allegiance.

If there were Tweets in the old days, which people from history might have sent these Tweets?

"I just picked up my Nobel Prize. They thought I looked positively radiant." (Marie Curie who won Nobel Prizes for her work on radioactivity, and eventually died from exposure to radiation).

"I'm thinking of opening a cake store. It'll make a killing." (Marie Antoinette, after making her supposed remark—"Let them eat cake"—when told that many French Revolutionists did not have enough bread to eat. She and many others were killed in the revolution).

"Has anybody got a more creative way to say 87 years?" (Abraham Lincoln when writing his Gettysburg Address in 1863, and using the phrase, "Four score and seven years ago," to indicate the-then 87 years since the founding of the country in 1776).

"Why did everyone else write so small? Now I look like a jerk." (John Hancock commenting on his big signature on the Declaration of Independence).

Who's buried in Grant's Tomb? (The answer is not as easy as one might think)

Grant's Tomb, on Riverside Drive in New York City, is an impressive monument to U.S. President Ulysses Grant.

You might remember that favorite quiz question asked by Groucho Marx, "Who's buried in Grant's Tomb"—but the obvious answer of Ulysses Grant is only half right. That's because Grant's wife Julia is there, too.

And technically, NOBODY is buried in Grant's Tomb. Ulysses and Julia are entombed above ground and not buried there.

How many numbers have the same amount of letters in their name as their meaning?

Of all the numbers, there is only one that has the same number of letters in its name as its meaning.

That is the number four which has four letters in its name.

ALL other numbers, when you spell them out, have a different number of letters in their name than their meaning, such as one has three letters, two has three letters, three has five letters, five has four letters, six has three letters, and so on and on.

Why were all the phones in America shut off on purpose one afternoon?

It was on Aug. 4, 1922 that all telephone service across America was shut down. The reason:

It was to honor the memory of Alexander Graham Bell. Bell, the man credited with being telephone's inventor, had died at age 75 on Aug. 2, 1922, and his funeral was taking place on Aug. 4.

It was during his funeral that phone companies suspended all telephone service.

Where's the highest waterfall in the world—and how far does the water fall?

The world's highest waterfall is the Angel Falls in Venezuela. Water drops there over 3,200 feet—or almost six times the height of the Washington Monument.

The Angel Falls got their name not from any association with their height being close to the angels, but from an American pilot, Jimmy Angel, who discovered them in 1933.

When Angel died in 1956, his ashes were scattered over the falls named after him.

One more amazing fact about the Angel Falls. The Empire State Building is 1,250 feet high. The Angel Falls are 2,000 feet higher than that. That's a big drop of water.

What are some contradictions in baseball terms?

Manager Casey Stengel once said, "Baseball is a funny game," and here are some examples:

If a batted ball hits the foul line or the foul pole, it's a fair ball.

The right-hand batter's box is on the left-field side of the plate, while the left-hand batter's box is on the right-field side of the plate.

If a batter walks with the bases loaded he's credited with a run BATTED in.

The word strike means to hit an object, but in baseball, strike is used when a batter swings and misses, or in the case of a called strike, doesn't swing at all.

It's lawful to steal.

Spring training starts in winter, in February.

If a batter fails to get a hit in two out of every three at bats all year, he's a star because a .333 batting average is considered very good.

Did a little girl play a part in the assassination of a U.S. president?

President William McKinley, a native of Ohio, always wore the state flower of Ohio—a scarlet carnation—in his lapel as a good luck charm.

In 1901, McKinley went to Buffalo to give a speech. In the reception line to meet the president was a little girl who told McKinley how pretty the flower in his lapel was. McKinley, taken by the girl's sweetness, asked her if she'd like it. Of course, she said yes. McKinley gave the flower to the little girl.

So, there McKinley stood, ready to greet more people—but without his lucky carnation. Soon, a man with a revolver got in the receiving line and fatally shot President McKinley.

Some say McKinley giving away his lucky charm had nothing to do with his assassination. But there are others who say if only McKinley hadn't given that lucky charm away, history might have been different.

They aren't well-remembered today, but what major events in U.S. history were Charles Guiteau and Leon Czolgosz responsible for?

Those involved in the assassination of two U.S. presidents are well-remembered—John Wilkes Booth, in the assassination of Abraham Lincoln, and Lee Harvey Oswald in the assassination of John Kennedy.

But pretty much forgotten in history were the assassins of two other assassinated presidents, James Garfield and William McKinley.

It was Charles Guiteau, described as a disappointed office seeker, who was the person who shot and killed President James Garfield, and it was Leon Czolgosc, described as an anarchist, who was the assassin of President McKinley.

At the end of World War I, why didn't any newspaper run a headline that said "World War I is Over"?

World War I was a war that had its name changed. During World War I and for 21 years after it, the war was not called World War I. It was simply called "The World War" because the second World War hadn't occurred yet. The war was also sometimes referred to as "The Great War."

In 1939, when the second World War started, it was called World War II, and the first World War then had its name changed to World War I.

Time magazine has made the claim that they were the first to put the Roman numerals on the two world wars, and they say they came up with the names World War II and World War I.

What mistake did the New York Museum of Modern Art make when they displayed a painting by Henri Matisse?

It was embarrassing for the prestigious New York Museum of Modern Art.

In 1961, they hung a Matisse painting—Le Bateau—upside down for 47 days until someone noticed it was upside down.

The mistake was finally caught by a New York stockbroker who notified a guard. The next day the museum turned the painting right-side up.

Surprise—what's the most crowded U.S. state—the one with the most people per square mile?

The most crowded U.S. state is not the one with the most population—but the one with the most people per square mile. And that state is New Jersey.

New Jersey has over 1,200 people per square mile—making it the most densely populated state in the nation. By contrast, the state with the most population, California, has just 239 people per square mile.

If you're looking for the least-crowded state, that place, by a wide margin, is Alaska with just over one person per square mile.

Why is golf called golf?

There's an old folktale that golf got its name from the initials of Gentlemen Only, Ladies Forbidden.

While ladies were forbidden to play at some golf courses in the old days—and even in modern times—that story about golf's name coming from Gentlemen Only Ladies Forbidden is not true.

So, how did golf get its name? Golf is a Dutch word meaning a club with which to hit a ball, and the sport took its name from that.

Which U.S. presidents never went to college?

Surprisingly, nine U.S. presidents never attended college.

And, among those presidents who never went to college were two of the greatest presidents: Neither George Washington or Abraham Lincoln ever attended college.

The other presidents who never went to college were Andrew Jackson, Martin Van Buren, Zachary Taylor, Millard Fillmore, Andrew Johnson, Grover Cleveland—and one 20th century president, Harry Truman.

Truman, president from 1945 to 1953, was the last president who never went to college.

There are 8 U.S. states whose names start with a letter that no other state's name starts with. What are those states?

Those states are:

Delaware, Florida, Georgia, Hawaii, Louisiana, Pennsylvania, Rhode Island and Utah.

Did turkeys get their name because they came from the country of Turkey?

Despite their name, turkeys did not come from Turkey, and in fact, turkeys are native only to the North American continent.

There were never any turkeys in Turkey until they were brought there from America.

So, how did turkeys get their name?

Turkeys were misnamed by English settlers in America. They thought the birds looked something like guinea hens from Turkey, so they called them turkeys—really a wrong name. The turkey is an entirely separate All-American species.

In fact, Benjamin Franklin wanted the turkey—instead of the eagle—to be the American symbol.

What was the longest war ever fought?

The longest war was the so-called Hundred Years War between England and France which actually lasted more than 100 years. It lasted 116 years, from 1337 to 1453.

France essentially won the war, as England lost Normandy to France and other footholds on the European continent.

That was also the war that made Joan of Arc famous.

By what famous name do we know meat distributor Sam Wilson today?

A man named Sam Wilson was a meat distributor in Troy, N.Y., and during the War of 1812, he supplied meat for the Army. Sam was known around Troy as Uncle Sam Wilson and he stamped that name on his barrels of meat. At that time, the name Uncle Sam was not yet the nickname for the United States, but soldiers began saying, "Uncle Sam is feeding the Army"—and then, the fact that the "U" and "S" of Uncle Sam's initials were the same as the "U" and "S" of the United States' initials, made for a nice tie-in, and the phrase "Uncle Sam" soon became the nickname for the nation.

That was eventually made official by a Congressional resolution, and today there's a plaque in Troy, N.Y., saying Troy was the hometown of the real Uncle Sam—meat distributor Sam Wilson.

What necessity did race car driver Ray Harroun add to our automobiles?

It's funny how ideas start. Take rear-view mirrors on cars. You'd think rear-view mirrors would have been an obvious necessity, but when automobiles were first made, they had no rear-view mirrors.

In the early days of auto racing, since there were no rear-view mirrors, cars had a driver plus a second person in the car whose job was to look behind, and tell the driver who was coming up on him and on which side.

Then in the 1911 Indianapolis 500-mile auto race, driver Ray Harroun had an idea. To lighten his car and make it go faster, he decided he'd drive alone. But who would look out behind for him?

Harroun invented the idea of the rear-view mirror for cars. He put one on his car, and soon other cars—race cars and regular cars—had rear-view mirrors, too.

Incidentally, Harroun won that 1911 Indy 500 with his then-revolutionary rear-view mirror.

Which U.S. president spent much of his term in bed?

After giving a long speech outdoors on a cold, blustery day in Washington on Inauguration Day in 1841, William Henry Harrison caught a bad cold which turned into pneumonia and sent him to bed.

His pneumonia proved fatal. He died just 31 days after his inauguration.

Harrison was president for only one month, and spent much of that month in bed.

How did H.J. Heinz of ketchup fame literally sink his competition?

In the early days of his company, Henry John Heinz faced a real problem. Three brothers not related to Henry but whose last names were also Heinz, started a competing company in Henry's hometown of Pittsburgh, and called their company, Heinz.

The brothers also hired away the man who designed Henry's labels, making their products look virtually the same. "You can't stop us," the three brothers wrote Henry. "We're just using our last name, like you do." Today such a thing would probably bring an unfair-business lawsuit. But this was the 1880s, and no suit was ever filed.

Then, fortune smiled on Henry. The three brothers couldn't pay their bank loans, and all their company assets were put up for sale. Henry went to the auction and bought everything—machinery, containers, all their products—and put them on a barge.

He then had that large barge towed out to the middle of Pittsburgh's Allegheny River, and sank the barge—literally sinking his competition.

What's the fastest-running 2-legged animal in the world?

The fastest-running 2-legged animal is, perhaps surprisingly, the ostrich. There are places that have ostrich races. Ostriches can reach 40 mph in speed.

Fastest-running 4-legged animal, by the way, is the cheetah which can reach speeds of 70 mph.

Fastest a human can run over a distance of 100 meters is about 23 mph.

Why do we use the words left and right in politics— why do we say left-wing and right-wing?

The words left and right in politics originated in the French legislature in the 1700s when liberal delegates just happened to seat themselves to the left of the speaker and conservative delegates just happened to seat themselves to the right of the speaker.

That's where the tradition started of referring to people's political views as left or right.

Although that custom was originally used only in France, it spread around the world and is used in many countries today.

Before Alaska and Hawaii, which were the last 3 U.S. states to enter the Union?

It's interesting to note that at the beginning of the last century, in 1901, the U.S. had only 45 states.

Then came five new states in the 1900s, with Alaska and Hawaii the 49th and 50th states, being admitted to the Union in 1959. The 46th state was Oklahoma, admitted to the Union in 1907 and the 47th and 48th states were New Mexico and Arizona, admitted to the Union in 1912.

Why didn't George Washington have a Christmas tree in his home?

It may be surprising to learn that virtually nobody in America had Christmas trees in their homes or offices until some 50 years after George Washington's time.

It wasn't until the mid-1800s that Christmas trees began to be prevalent in America. The idea of indoor, decorated Christmas trees originated in Germany, and in the mid-1800s a large number of German immigrants began coming to America, and they brought their custom of Christmas trees with them.

Christmas trees were also popularized in the mid-1800s by Germany's Prince Albert when he married England's Queen Victoria and brought the custom to England. A picture of their first Christmas tree had a big influence in the U.S., and furthered their use in America.

Which 2 very well-known countries in the world are smaller than Central Park in New York City?

There are two countries in the world—two independent, sovereign nations—that are smaller than Central Park.

Central Park in New York is 1.3 square miles, but the nation of Monaco in Europe where movie star Grace Kelly was once a princess and where the famous Monte Carlo is, has a land area of less than one square mile. Little Monaco, by the way, is a full-fledged member of the United Nations.

The other country smaller than Central Park is the Vatican, which is a sovereign nation and could be a U.N. member if they chose. The Vatican, like Monaco, is less than one square mile.

Which prestigious college named itself after its football coach?

There's a well-known and well-thought of college in upstate New York, in Hamilton, N.Y., that used to be called Madison University.

But in 1890, they changed the name of the college to the name of their football coach, Sam Colgate, and became Colgate University.

Sam Colgate was a member of the family that makes Colgate toothpaste and his family was a big benefactor to the school. Sam Colgate himself became the football coach there for several years.

Colgate University remains today the only college named after its football coach.

What are the answers to these riddles sent to us by our radio listeners?

Why didn't Cinderella make the basketball team?
(She ran away from the Ball).

Why couldn't the dog bark?
(He was a hush puppy).

What did one earthquake say to another?
(It's not my fault).

What did the lawyer name his baby daughter?
(Sue).

What did one candle-light say to the other?
(Do you want to go out tonight?).

Why did the football coach go to the bank?
(To get his quarter back).

Why do hummingbirds hum?
(They don't know the words).

Why did the pony speak softly?
(He was a little hoarse).

Why didn't the sesame seed lose at the casino gambling table?
(Because he was on a roll).

When the fog lifts in Southern California, what do you see?
(U. C. L. A.).

What kind of coffee did they serve on the Titanic?
(Sanka).

What did the man say when he threw his watch across the room?
(My, how time flies).

Why was the young ant confused?
(All his uncles were ants).

Why did the boy never tell anyone that he ate the glue?
(His lips were sealed).

In which war did soldiers arrive by taxi cabs to fight a battle?

Strange things often happen in war, and here's one of the strangest.

In the Battle of the Marne in World War I, French soldiers arrived for the battle not on foot or by airplane or by military vehicles—but by taxi cabs.

The French general in charge of the battle took over all the taxis in Paris to get the soldiers to the front. Thousands of soldiers came by taxi to fight that major battle.

Before they started fighting, we wonder if the soldiers tipped the drivers.

What man lost more than a presidential election?

Horace Greeley, the newspaper publisher who achieved fame when he popularized the saying, "Go West, young man," ran for U.S. president against Ulysses Grant in 1872.

During the fall election campaign, Greeley became ill and began facing severe personal financial problems. In late October, just before the election, Greeley's wife who had also been ill, died. On Nov. 4, Election Day, Greeley lost the election to Grant. On Nov. 29, Greeley, himself, died.

It was a tragic end for Horace Greeley who lost his wife, his money, his presidential election, and his own life in a two-month period.

In what unlikely way did Snowflake, Ariz., get its name?

If you tell this story to someone, they'll probably think you're kidding, but it's absolutely true.

There's a town in Arizona named Snowflake, but that's not the unbelievable part. It does snow in parts of Arizona.

What's unbelievable is that the town of Snowflake, northeast of Phoenix, was named for two guys named Snow and Flake. Honest.

Mormons settled the town in 1877 and sent church member William Flake to get it organized. The man in charge of Mormon colonization was Erastus Snow. Early residents honored Erastus Snow and William Flake and named the town Snowflake.

Today, Snowflake, Ariz., has a varied population of about 5,000 and there's a plaque there that says this town was founded by Erastus Snow and William Flake   That seems too good to be true, but it is true.

Which major pro sports teams' nicknames don't end in "s"?

In major league baseball, there are two such teams, the Boston Red Sox and Chicago White Sox.

In the National Basketball Association, there are the Miami Heat, Oklahoma City Thunder, Orlando Magic and Utah Jazz.

In the National Hockey League, there are the Colorado Avalanche, Minnesota Wild, Seattle Kraken and Tampa Bay Lightning.

There are none in the National Football League—all their nicknames end in "s".

What is it about left-handers and the presidency?

It's an amazing fact that defies statistical probability.

Although only about 10-to-15 percent of the overall U.S. population is left-handed, incredibly, about **70 PERCENT** of all U.S. presidents from 1974 to 2016 have been left-handed.

The presidents from 1974 to 2016 have been Gerald Ford, Jimmy Carter, Ronald Reagan, George H.W. Bush, Bill Clinton, George W. Bush and Barack Obama. Of those seven presidents, five have been left-handed—Ford, Reagan, George H.W. Bush, Clinton and Obama—five of the seven.

That not only defies statistical probability, but does so by a fantastic margin.

Which U.S. state has counties named Crisp, Bacon and Coffee?

Not only does the state of Georgia have counties named Crisp, Bacon and Coffee, but there were actually three men with those last names that the counties were named after.

Crisp County was named for Charles Crisp who was a U.S. Congressman from Georgia and Speaker of the House of Representatives from 1891 to 1895.

Bacon County was named after Augustus Bacon who was a U.S. senator from Georgia in the late 1800s.

And, Coffee County was named for General John Coffee who, besides his military career, was a Georgia state legislator and member of the U.S. House of Representatives in the early 1800s.

This delicious oddity of three counties in one state being named Crisp, Bacon and Coffee is made even more interesting by the fact that Bacon and Coffee Counties are right next to each other, and Crisp County is not far away in southern Georgia.

What do the "O" and "K" stand for in the expression "OK"?

There are several theories on where OK came from, but most word historians believe it was popularized in our language from the hometown of U.S. president Martin Van Buren.

Van Buren, elected president in 1836, was from the little upstate New York town of Kinderhook, which he affectionately called Old Kinderhook.

During his re-election campaign in 1840, his supporters took the initials of Old Kinderhook—OK—and formed the OK Club to raise money for Van Buren. They also gave Van Buren the nickname "OK," coining the expression to mean he was "good" or "all right."

Then a strange thing happened.

Gradually, OK began to enter our language for meaning anyone or anything was all right, and eventually OK came into wide usage. But just think: If Van Buren had been from some other town, we might not be saying OK today.

It's amazing now how many times people say OK every day. It would be interesting to start counting how many times you hear yourself and other people say OK.

What 2 words have been seen so often on movie screens in movie history?

The answer to this question are two words that have appeared with so many feature films over the years.

Those two words are "The End"—and that is a fitting last question-and-answer for this book, because, as they have said in the movies, this is "**The End**." Hope you enjoyed it.